Managing teams in secondary schools

373.12/B

T   for the
m   nges for
th   r teams.

M   achers
wh   hers in
sec   in the
ma   ges the
Act   within
that   th the
natu   nd of
the s   icular
at te   and
prob   staff
deve   the
mana
   Pri   dary
schoo   erest
to any

Les Be   ore
enterin   els.
He has   on
educati

Managing teams in secondary schools

Les Bell

London and New York

First published 1992
by Routledge
11 New Fetter Lane, London EC4P 4EE

Simultaneously published in the USA and Canada
by Routledge
a division of Routledge, Chapman and Hall Inc.
29 West 35th Street, New York, NY 10001

Typeset in Garamond by LaserScript, Mitcham, Surrey
Printed and bound in Great Britain by
Biddles Ltd, Guildford and King's Lynn

A catalogue reference for this title is available from the British Library.

ISBN 0–415–03217–2
   0–415–08042–8

Library of Congress Cataloging in Publication Data

Bell, Les, 1942–
  Managing teams in secondary schools / by Les Bell.
    p. cm. – (Educational management series)
  Includes bibliographical references and index.
  ISBN 0–415–03217–2. – ISBN 0–415–08042–8 (pbk.)
  1. School management teams–Great Britain. 2. School management and
organization–Great Britain. 3. Education, Secondary–Great Britain.
  4. Leadership. I. Title. II. Series.
  LB2806.3.B45 1992
  373.12′00941–dc20   92–2802
                                                          CIP

Contents

List of figures   vii
List of tables   ix
Foreword   xi
Acknowledgements   xiii

1 **The context of secondary school management**   1

2 **Management for effective schools**   13

3 **Leadership and management in secondary schools**   28

4 **Staff teams and their management**   44

5 **Developing the school**   58

6 **The staff team: Its priorities and their management**   73

7 **Communication in schools**   84

8 **Curriculum profiles and job descriptions**   107

9 **Staff appraisal and the secondary school team**   125

10 **Conclusion: Development, change and stability**   141

Bibliography   169
Index   174

Figures

5.1 The school development cycle   62

5.2 Factors influencing a school's development plan   67

6.1 Managing priorities   80

10.1 Staff appraisal and school development   142

10.2 A force field model – present situation   154

Tables

4.1 Teamwork   45

4.2 The benefits of teamwork in the school   46

4.3 Developing the staff team   53

5.1 A staffing audit   65

6.1 Establishing effective targets   77

6.2 Stages in effective delegation   82

7.1 Are communications effective in your school?   87

7.2 Making communication work   88

7.3 Body language   90

7.4 Purposes of meetings   98

7.5 The organisation of a meeting   104

8.1 Techniques for producing a curriculum profile   109

8.2 Curriculum profile for individual members of a department   110

8.3 A curriculum related staff profile   112

8.4 A school profile   114

8.5 Job description   117

8.6 A job description and specification for a secondary school deputy headteacher   120

9.1 A checklist for observing a teacher's classroom performance   136

9.2 The benefits of staff appraisal in schools   137

9.3 Preparation for staff appraisal   138

10.1 Some further strategies for staff development in schools   144

10.2 Choosing a strategy for implementing staff development   146

10.3 Reviewing staff development strategies   149

10.4 Ways of collecting information   156

10.5 Action grid   159

Foreword

Les Bell has an outstanding reputation as a writer of books on educational management that are unfussy, easy to read, knowledgeable and, above all, of immense help to the practising teacher. This book is no exception. *Managing Teams in Secondary Schools* sits worthily alongside his earlier *Management Skills in Primary Schools* in this series. There is no doubt that, in the present educational climate of rapid change, the management of secondary schools must undergo a radical reappraisal. While headteachers are ultimately responsible to their governing bodies for the conduct and success of their schools, they can no longer achieve high standards by exhortation or charismatic leadership. Schools, like many other public and private institutions, now depend for their success on the active participation of the staff as a whole. This is not a simple matter of effective delegation, as it was thought to be not so long ago. Schools must be a co-partnership of staff at all levels.

This book addresses itself, not merely to team leaders as a tier in management, but to team members including those in leadership roles. In effect it is a book for every secondary school teacher, since every one is today not only a member of a team, but a contributor to decision-making within that team. Whether or not a secondary school describes its management style as collegiate or corporate is of little consequence. The truth of the matter is that, without the sharing of real responsibility, a school will find difficulty in coping with the pressures of today.

Les Bell avoids the presentation of systems of management that, however worthy, are unmanageable. While everything in this book will contribute to the making of the effective school, readers may choose for implementation whatever they regard as both most pressing for their role in the institution and most realisable within the constraints of time and energy. It is also a must for any aspirant to promotion. There has never been a time in education when knowledge about the full range of management skills and roles was of such vital importance to teachers of all levels of seniority.

Cyril Poster

Acknowledgements

This book is dedicated to all my friends and colleagues in secondary education, many of whom have contributed directly or indirectly by sharing their experiences with me and by being active participants in many management courses. I am especially grateful to those students on B.Phil and M.Ed educational management courses who have contributed so much to the development of my own thinking on management practice. Recently we have all benefited from the insights of David Halpin who joined the Education Department of the University of Warwick in 1990. Working with him has sharpened my own perceptions about secondary school management.

Much that is written here has been influenced strongly by Kingsley Bungard of the Management Consulting Group, Barclays Venture Centre, University of Warwick, with whom I have worked closely on many management development projects. Liz Tomkins, headteacher of Kingsbury Comprehensive School, Warwickshire commented extensively on the first draft of this book. I am extremely grateful for her help. Cyril Poster has been a demanding and insightful series editor. This volume has benefited greatly from his advice. To Barbara Gray, who typed and retyped from my manuscripts, I owe my thanks for her industry and tolerance.

Les Bell

Chapter 1

The context of secondary school management

This book is for those teachers who have management responsibility in secondary schools. It provides an analysis of those responsibilities and, at the same time, offers a wide range of practical guidelines for the development of effective strategies to enable the manager in the secondary school to cope with the changes and challenges that now confront all of us in education. The first basic premise of the book is that all teachers in secondary schools have a direct and developing part to play in the management of the school at some level. This may be as a member of a subject department or a faculty, a pastoral team, or a cross-curricular group such as that which is responsible for the Technical and Vocational Educational Initiative (TVEI) and its extension. It may be as a leader of such a group at the middle management level in the school or it may be as a member of the senior management of the school at deputy or headteacher level.

Clearly the responsibility for the overall management and administration of every school rests with the headteacher and the senior management team working with and through the governing body. This is immutable and will remain so in spite of the recent changes contained in the 1986 and 1988 Education Acts. Nevertheless, it is becoming increasingly clear that the whole staff of the school is expected to exercise greater collective responsibility for the content of the curriculum, the forms of assessment, the deployment and utilisation of resources, the routine decisions which are taken about children and the ways in which they are to be taught. This is a logical extension of the movement towards greater accountability in schools which began with the Great Debate on Education and the green paper, *Education in Schools: A Consultative Document* (HMSO 1977a). It is also a theme developed at length by HMI and summed up in their publication, *Education Observed 3: Good Teachers*, where it is argued that:

> teachers need to work together collectively to produce an atmosphere in the school which encourages children to respond in a positive and responsible fashion. . . . Reference to the importance of professional team work appears frequently in school reports. Typical is the comment . . .

'The members of staff work as a team so that they can offer leadership and guidance in areas of the curriculum that might present difficulties to individual teachers. In this way weaknesses and omissions are assessed and, as far as is possible, remedied. These comments emphasise the importance of professional teamwork for maximum curricular strength and mutual support.

(DES 1985b: paras. 13–30)

The need for effective school management to be based on teamwork within schools is the second basic premise of this book. Schools are not made up of a large number of autonomous individuals acting independently of each other. Pupils are grouped in classes, sets, streams, year groups, houses, teams and in many other ways. They are expected to act as a group rather than as individuals when they are thus organised. The same is true of teachers who may belong to departments, teams or a variety of other units within which they are expected to act, to a greater or lesser degree, in concert with colleagues. The effective management of these groups of teachers is vital to the well-being of the school and for the education of the children within the school. The responsibility for this task falls to all teachers.

The Education (School Teachers' Pay and Conditions) Order (DES 1987a) reminds us that the main professional grade (now standard grade) teacher will be responsible for:

- advising and co-operating with the headteacher and other teachers . . . on the preparation and development of courses of study, teaching materials, teaching programmes, methods of teaching and assessment and pastoral arrangements;
- contributing to the selection for appointment and professional development of other teachers;
- co-ordinating or managing the work of other teachers;
- taking such part as may be required . . . in the review, development and management of activities relating to the curriculum, organisation and pastoral functions of the school.

(DES 1987a: Schedule 3, paras 3.1–3.12, p. 5)

The conditions of employment for headteachers contain even more specific managerial elements. These include:

- representing the school in its formal relationships with the local education authority (LEA) and governors;
- formulating the overall aims of the school;
- participating in the selection and appointment of staff;
- organising the implementation of the national curriculum;
- reviewing the work and organisation of the school;
- evaluating standards of teaching and learning;

- ensuring that all staff have access to advice and training appropriate to their needs.

(DES 1987a: Schedule 1, paras 4.1–4.23, pp. 2–3)

These statements about the responsibilities of both headteachers and standard grade teachers echo those descriptions of good practice which were identified by HMI in *Good Teachers* (DES 1985b). The essential features are almost identical, stressing as they do, the nature of the wider responsibilities within schools that go far beyond work in classrooms. Such wider responsibilities involve working with colleagues and accepting some measure of accountability for that work. They also involve most teachers in the general management and organisation of the school in which they work. As Marland suggests:

> In England and Wales, despite some recent centralist tendencies, a significant proportion of the key decisions are made within the schools, often by teachers who hold posts of responsibility. This elevates the management skills of the teachers, as opposed to their pedagogical skills, into very great importance.

(Marland 1986: 1)

In spite of the reference to posts of responsibility which now no longer exist, the fundamental message is clear. Teachers at all levels in schools have management responsibilities as part of their everyday duties. These responsibilities are not carried out in isolation but involve working with and through colleagues. The management of this process, the management of teams of teachers in schools, is crucial to the provision of a good education for our children. As Styan has stated:

> Teachers *have the right* to expect well-managed schools which provide the conditions for good teaching and learning. Heads and senior staff have the major responsibility for creating these conditions.

(Styan 1989a)

The creation of these conditions, however, is a shared responsibility at all levels of the school.

SECONDARY SCHOOL MANAGEMENT IN A NEW ERA

It is clear to any teacher in any school in the last decade of the twentieth century that education is entering a new era. It has been suggested that the combined effects of economy, demography and ideology have produced a situation in which the management of schools requires new sets of under-standings and skills (Simkins and Thomas 1987). The worldwide recession caused by the oil crisis in the early 1970s exacerbated problems of low economic growth and rising unemployment in the United Kingdom. As a result all public sector activities faced increasing demands for greater economies, improved efficiency and better value for money.

Education was no exception to this. Indeed the pressures for all educational institutions to examine their own internal efficiency were made even greater by the decline in pupil numbers coinciding with a growing concern about the rising number of unemployed and elderly people who were placing increasing demands on health and social services. There needed to be a shift in resources away from those devoted primarily to the young, towards those from which the elderly and the unwaged were the main beneficiaries. The argument that declining pupil numbers might lead to a better pupil–teacher ratio was lost. Instead resource allocation in education became much more closely linked to notions of purpose and priority. Hence, resources were available for some developments – TVEI and in-service training for the introduction of the General Certificate of Secondary Education (GCSE) for example – but not for others.

At the same time ideological shifts in the political climate related to 'the perceived purpose of education, the autonomy of its teaching force and the perceived propriety of using certain techniques for evaluating educational activity' (Simkins and Thomas 1987: 8) have led to a situation in which education is being required to take a greater account of the needs of the industrial and commercial sectors, possibly at the expense of a more liberal approach to education. Consequently science and technology in the National Curriculum receive a greater emphasis than they did in the curriculum of most schools in the past. There is now a challenge to the traditional autonomy of the teacher over the choice of curriculum content and teaching style. Procedures are being established to measure the performance of the education system and the levels of achievement of children by setting basic national standards. These issues find expression in the National Curriculum. They also provide significant professional and managerial challenges for teachers at all levels in secondary education.

As these challenges have emerged, approaches to the management of secondary schools have changed. During the 1960s and early 1970s the general trend in secondary education was towards the creation of larger schools (Bell and Maher 1986). Prior to that, in the small schools that tended to be the norm, a relatively autocratic style of headship was expected from secondary school headteachers. With a teaching staff of about twenty and one deputy, such an autocratic style could flourish and go largely unchallenged. Such schools were small enough and the curriculum was sufficiently narrow and relatively unchanging to enable the institution to be controlled by one individual. As schools became larger and the curriculum became more complex and less static, such an approach to the management of secondary schools was inappropriate and difficult to sustain.

New approaches to school management became necessary as pupil numbers increased and LEAs took the opportunity to seek economies of scale by creating large schools as they reorganised to cope with comprehensive secondary schooling. The new institutions were too big to be managed by any one individual acting alone. Many of the people appointed to senior positions within them had previously been headteachers in their own right. New forms of examination within the Certificate of Secondary Education (CSE) were being developed and teachers were coming into contact with types of pupils with whom they were not familiar. On top of all this the school leaving age was due to be raised to sixteen years, thus adding a new dimension to both organisational and curricular structures in many schools.

Schools were faced with a new range of problems. One set of solutions was to delegate responsibility to members of staff for specialist areas of subject, pastoral and organisational aspects of the school. This approach was reinforced by various pay awards which sought to differentiate between teachers at different levels within the school organisation. Headteachers tended, therefore, to create senior management teams. These often started with two deputies who had responsibility for the pastoral and the academic areas of the school's activities. This is not to say that these two areas were either clearly understood or clearly delineated. Confusion about responsibilities often occurred, made worse when many schools found themselves with three deputies. What was the third deputy to do? A common answer to this question can be found in the growth of deputy heads who were responsible for day-to-day organisation and administration. This often meant 'doing the cover rota'. Nevertheless, the team approach to school management began to emerge.

The second phase in the establishment of management structures in large secondary schools came with the development and extension of middle management functions. Heads of subject departments had existed for some time. Heads of pastoral teams became established with the growth of large comprehensive schools. It was a fairly simple progression, therefore, to delegate some of the senior management responsibilities to the holders of these posts. The Houghton pay award, the need to establish career routes into more senior levels of the school organisation, and subsequent pressures on schools to extend and rethink their curricular provision and to accept an even wider pastoral remit reinforced such developments.

In recent years a third phase has begun under the influence of TVEI, the growing emphasis on vocationalism, the introduction of information technology across the curriculum, and the development of new forms of pupil assessment and record keeping. This phase has seen the emergence of the role of the co-ordinator. This role has tended to be cross-curricular in nature and has often involved having general responsibility for resource management in a way that was uncommon for heads of department or pastoral teams. As headteachers and their senior staff have to accept new responsibilities and new roles, so do those in middle management positions.

They may find themselves with greater subject or pastoral commitments as well as a broader, school-wide responsibility for functions such as resource management.

These changes in approaches to management inside the school are mirrored by changes in the predominant management style in the external environment of most secondary schools. As Blanchard *et al.* (1989) put it, there has been a shift from management by consensus to management by accountability. In the period from 1944 to the late 1980s the management of the education system was carried out by the DES, LEAs and the schools in terms of a partnership in which each partner could offer advice to the others but could operate only through influence. For example, the governing body of a school could not impose its views on the content of the curriculum or on the teaching of it within that school. The same was true of both the LEA and the Government. Advice could be given and certain courses of action such as giving a greater emphasis to science within the curriculum could be encouraged. Changes might take place only by agreement. In short:

> the educational environment encouraged by the 1944 Education Act was one in which consensus was the overriding principle.
>
> (Blanchard *et al.* 1989: 5)

As a result of the two education acts in the late 1980s the situation is now very different. The 1986 Education Act reduced the numbers of LEA governors on school governing bodies and increased parental representation. It also gave governors the power to modify an LEA's curriculum policy statement and exercise limited control over the school's budget. The same act gave, for the first time, a clear indication that governors were accountable to parents for their stewardship of the school. It required them to furnish parents with an annual report dealing with the work of the governing body during the year and also to hold an annual parents' meeting at the school to discuss the report. The 1988 Education Reform Act (ERA) made even more drastic and significant changes.

This act introduced the National Curriculum with three core subjects and seven foundation subjects. It established a National Curriculum Council to advise the Secretary of State on curriculum matters and a Schools Examination and Assessment Council to oversee the assessment of pupils. Religious education has now to be provided under an agreed syllabus and a wholly or broadly Christian act of worship has to take place in schools for all children each day. Parents must be informed about the ways in which the school is approaching the National Curriculum; assessment and testing and the provision of religious education and a complaints procedure must be established to enable parents to ensure that the terms of the act are being carried out. Open enrolment has come into force to compel schools to admit all pupils whose parents wish them to attend that school provided that it is not full. Governing bodies of schools of more than 200 pupils now must assume responsibility for the school's finances, while those with fewer than 200 may also be given delegated budgets. Governors can decide staffing levels and make recommendations about appointments and dismissals. They may also seek for their school to opt out of LEA control by applying to the Secretary of State for grant-maintained status. These are all significant elements in the move towards management by accountability since each school now has to accept responsibility for:

- implementing the National Curriculum through programmes of study linked to specific attainment targets;
- appointing, supporting, promoting and managing teaching and ancillary staff;
- managing its own budget within the LEA scheme of financial delegation;
- publishing information to parents on these matters and being accountable to them and to the LEA for its performance.

It requires the highest level of management skill to cope with these demands. The central importance of a high level of such skills in school has long been recognised. It was argued in the white paper, *Teaching Quality*, that:

> Headteachers, and other . . . staff with management responsibilities within the schools, are of crucial importance. Only if they are effective managers of their teaching staffs and the material resources available to them, as well as possessing the qualities needed for effective educational leadership, can schools offer their pupils the quality of education which they have the right to expect.
>
> (DES 1983: para. 83)

If this is to be achieved in the present context of management by accountability then each school has to have staff with the skills and abilities to organise and develop the professional capacity of all those people working in the school. Senior staff in schools will need to accept an even more managerial role, although this will have to be firmly rooted in their professional knowledge and experience. Headteachers, in particular, will spend more time on what has been called the chief executive role which will encompass management, administrative, financial and evaluative skills as well as professional expertise in education. If these functions are to be carried out successfully the chief executive will need to be able to call upon the skill and expertise of colleagues both individually and collectively. The senior staff in the school will have to be blended to form an effective management team. At the same time, those in middle management positions will find that their roles have expanded because of the changes in the work of senior managers in their schools. Above all, middle managers in schools will need the ability to lead and manage a team of professional colleagues within the new framework that has been created by the recent legislation.

This framework will itself help to determine the nature of the management tasks that senior and middle managers in secondary schools and their teams are going to deal with in the future. For example, the National Curriculum Council's (NCC) information pack, number 1 makes it quite clear that the National Curriculum – in the words of the first overhead transparency 'Why a National Curriculum?' – is intended to:

- give a clear incentive for the weaker schools to catch up with the best and the best will be challenged to do even better;
- provide teachers with detailed and precise objectives;
- provide parents with clear, accurate information;
- ensure continuity and progression from one year to another, from one school to another;
- help teachers to concentrate on the task of getting the best possible results from each individual child.

These things will not just happen. They need to be managed at a variety of different levels within the school since they have implications for the organisation of teaching and learning within each classroom, within each department and at school level. There are also wider implications related to appropriate forms of teaching and learning, the provision of guidance and counselling, the nature and form of information collected and transmitted about pupils, the provision for pupils with special educational needs, and equal opportunities. Furthermore, the National Curriculum involves schools in examining relationships between different areas of the same school, between secondary schools and their partner primary schools, and between schools and parents. Much of this is not made explicit in the information pack but is, nevertheless, clear to any teacher with the responsibility for managing a team in any secondary school.

There are some immediate implications to which the attention of teachers with management responsibility in secondary schools is drawn in the first information pack. These take two forms. The first is a series of questions:

- How can we ensure that all pupils in years 7 to 9 study all the core and other foundation subjects for a reasonable period of time?
- How will the curriculum for these years need to change during the next three years?
- What are the staffing implications of these changes?
- What other resources are needed?
- How do we ensure that all staff feel involved in the National Curriculum?
- How should we inform parents about the National Curriculum?

(National Curriculum Council 1989: OHT 21)

These questions draw attention to detailed processes of curriculum management, as well as to the management of staff and other resources including staff and pupil time. They also lead to an examination of the ways in which staff are consulted about the work of the school and are involved in the decision-making, planning and implementation processes in their schools, faculties, departments and teams. Implied in all this is the need to establish procedures that will ensure that all staff play an active part in the management of the curriculum and also have access to the necessary staff development in order to enable them to continue so to do.

The second set of implications takes the form of actions that teachers will need to carry out in order to implement the National Curriculum. These relate specifically to teachers of science and mathematics but they are relevant to all teachers, since everyone will need to be involved in carrying out these actions for his or her own subject. The actions are:

(a) extract relevant information from the reports of the working groups and NCC advice to the Secretary of State;
(b) study the statutory orders for subjects when they are published and also the non-statutory guidance;
(c) compare the statutory orders with existing teaching schemes and draw up a plan of action to ensure that all the prescribed programmes of study are taught;
(d) prepare and adapt resource material;
(e) plan for recording pupils' progress;
(f) prepare for continuous assessment of pupils.

(Adapted from National Curriculum Council 1989: OHT 22)

Any teacher will recognise just how time-consuming the processes outlined will be and how much effort in many schools has already gone into profiling and other forms of recording pupils' progress in the continuous assessment related to GCSEs. What is not recognised here, however, is the likely impact of the statutory orders on the work of many schools. Coping with them will require much more than a simple adaptation of existing teaching programmes and a modification of readily available resources. At the same time the assumption is made here that all secondary schools have subject specialists available to do this work. A study of the match between teachers' professional qualifications and the subjects that they were teaching concluded that:

Mismatch occurs more widely than just in so-called shortage subjects . . . evidence suggests that mismatched teaching limits the pedagogical scope of the teaching and adversely affects the quality of work.

(Merson 1989: 181)

The detailed requirements of the National Curriculum will make such a situation even worse unless heads of departments working in conjunction with senior management teams can deploy the necessary resources in order to provide support and appropriate staff development for colleagues for whom mismatch is a problem. Staff teams in secondary schools and the resources available to them will require even more effective management in the light of the demands placed upon them by the National Curriculum.

Other significant changes introduced by the ERA also require an effective and co-ordinated management response from inside secondary schools. The move towards local resource management in schools is normally referred to by the inaccurate description of local management of schools (LMS) after the Coopers and Lybrand (1988) report for the DES. This nomenclature gives a primacy to resource management that hitherto had been reserved for the educational aims that schools sought to achieve. The formulation of these aims and what they might encompass will be examined in some detail in chapter 2. Suffice it to say here that schools must deploy the resources at their disposal in order to provide children with that to which they are now entitled. This is a broad and balanced curriculum which will promote spiritual, moral, cultural, mental and physical development and which will provide a preparation for the opportunities, responsibilities and experiences of adult life. If this is to be achieved then groups of teachers working with others, such as governors, have to take a range of decisions and make a variety of choices about the deployment and management of resources in their schools. This should not be done in isolation from an understanding of what their school is trying to achieve. The management of resources and the establishment of aims for the school can only be done effectively as part of a process of teamwork.

At the same time, coping with the demands of open enrolment, the existence of grant-maintained schools or city technology colleges in the neighbourhood, and learning to work with school governors in different and challenging ways will all require a team-based approach to school management that has not always been evident in some schools in the past. What Jones (1987) has called the *monarchic* approach to the management of schools, with its hint of autocracy and despotism, is now neither appropriate nor possible even at headteacher level. The bureaucratic form of management, still in evidence in many schools is, argues Jones, extremely difficult to sustain because of its emphasis on centralised control within the school and the belief that for each problem there exists one correct solution. Such an approach to school management tended to produce systems that were inflexible and slow to respond to changes, especially those which stem from the external environment (Poster 1976). We are now moving into an era when flexible and responsive management of schools is necessary to ensure that new challenges can be met and overcome. This means that power and responsibility has to be shared within the school. As this happens those teachers in middle management positions in secondary schools may detect that more is being required of them as they and their teams of colleagues play a more active role in school, departmental and team management.

This sharing has, by law, to be extended to stakeholders in the school such as governors and parents. One important element of the ERA is the increasing power given to governing bodies over finance, staffing, discipline and the implementation of the curriculum. This not only implies a changing relationship between teachers and governors, but *requires* such a change. Some argue that this change will be restricted to headteachers (Adams 1989) but as headteachers delegate responsibility to senior colleagues for finance, staff development and appraisal, the maintenance of sites and buildings, and various aspects of the academic and pastoral work of the school, such changes will have a much wider impact. Adams (1989) argues that new kinds of management teams will be needed within which leading professionals in the schools will co-operate with a disparate collection of individuals with wide experience of the outside world. In order to make such teams work for the benefit of the schools and the children, the skills necessary for effective team management need to be a crucial item on the agenda for all those involved in secondary school management. As Styan (1989b) maintains, the basic skills required for the successful management of schools have not changed. School management is essentially about people and how to work together to achieve specific goals. It is about balancing and reconciling the widely differing needs and expectations of those within the school in the light of the many forces outside the school that seek to influence its activities. The recent educational reforms have not changed this; rather they have served to emphasise the importance of such skills and to remind all of those concerned in school management of the need to exercise those skills effectively within a framework of professionals working together in co-operation with other stakeholders in the school community.

The context within which secondary schools have to be managed is changing as a result of the ways in which the education service has responded to developments in the wider society since the mid-1970s. Economic, demographic and ideological changes have produced pressures on schools to give greater emphasis to scientific, technological and vocational aspects of the curriculum. The introduction of a National Curriculum and related forms of assessing pupil progress has played a significant part in helping to shape the type of education that is now being offered to children. It has created a framework within which teachers have to be more accountable to governors, parents and the community at large for what happens in schools.

At the same time staff in schools are being required to accept an increased managerial responsibility. To a large extent this is a result of a broad range of policies intended to increase the effectiveness of the internal management of schools. This found its expression in the legislation affecting schools that was passed in the 1980s concerning teachers' conditions of service, the role of governors in the management of schools, and changes in the ways in which schools are resourced. Some senior managers devote time to resource management and to managing the external relationships of the school, including those mechanisms by which schools have to render themselves accountable. Other staff in the school, therefore, have to accept greater responsibility for its internal management. To do this effectively teams have to be established and developed to cope with a wide range of tasks, or the autonomy of the teacher in the classroom has to give way to a more collegial, co-operative approach to the management of the school.

How far this is recognised by all teachers and the extent to which they become involved in the work of their school above and beyond a direct concern for the pedagogical aspects of teaching depends, in part, on the organisation of their particular school and on the opportunities which that organisation offers for such involvement. It also depends on the individual teacher's understanding of the nature of management and of the relationship between what Styan (1989b) calls the basic skills of management and the work of teachers in secondary school teams. What management means within the broad context of secondary education, and how management practices may be identified, understood and applied, becomes the focal point of concern. This book sets out to try to illuminate that concern. What, then, are those skills to which Styan refers? The next chapter will seek to answer this question.

ACTIVITIES

1 List at least three ways in which the introduction of the National Curriculum has had an impact on you in your school.
2 Identify at least three significant changes that have taken place in your school as a result of LMS.
3 Examine how far the changing role of the governing body has had an impact on the management of your school.

Chapter 2

Management for effective schools

The skills to which Styan (1989b) directs our attention are associated with the ways in which schools are organised and with those functions that have to be performed in order to make schools effective. The basic form of organisation in secondary schools as identified by HMI is one in which there is:

> a head, and depending on the age range, . . . two or three deputy head-teachers and one or more members of staff on senior teacher scale. In many schools one deputy head had overall responsibility for pastoral care, another for curricular matters and, in schools with three deputies, the third often had responsibility for day-to-day organisation and administration . . . In all the schools, two broad kinds of responsibility formed the framework for the staffing structure; the majority of posts above scale one were allocated for responsibilities for parts of the curriculum . . . A smaller proportion was for pastoral care . . . Much depended on the effectiveness of the delegation of responsibilities to heads of department . . . and to those responsible for pastoral care.
>
> (DES 1988b: 75)

In spite of its now dated reference to scales this excerpt describes the form of management structure within which many teachers in secondary schools now find themselves working and will continue to work, albeit with certain modifications brought about by the need to respond to the Education Reform Act and related changes. Its emphasis on the centrality of the role of senior management and on the importance of effective delegation has much in common with the concluding section of that much quoted document, *Ten Good Schools* (DES 1977b) which recognised that, while schools vary in many different respects, what the best schools had in common was effective leadership and a climate conducive to growth:

> The schools see themselves as places designated for learning; they take trouble to make their philosophies explicit for themselves and to explain them to parents and pupils; the foundation of their work and corporate life is an acceptance of shared values.

Emphasis is laid on consultation, team work and participation but, without exception, the most important single factor in the success of these schools is the qualities of leadership of the head.

(DES 1977b: Section 8)

Two years later we find HMI arguing, in *Aspects of Secondary Education*, that:

The indications are that collective thinking and planning are difficult to achieve, even where there is appreciation of the need.

(DES 1979a: 263)

It is suggested that one of the major reasons for this state of affairs is lack of time. The discussion of policies, their translation into the planning of specific programmes of work in the classroom and their regular evaluation and assessment take more time than many teachers have at their disposal. This is especially true of those in middle management positions who have suffered from the inability of many schools to relate the allocation of non-teaching time to the special responsibilities which these teachers were expected to fulfil. The introduction of 1,265 hours of allocated time may have helped with this but the added pressures of current changes will have more than counteracted any such benefits.

HMI pointed out that the organisational complexities of schools can make it very difficult for teachers to understand with any degree of certainty the full programme of all the pupils that they teach. The same complexity makes meeting with colleagues, let alone understanding all the demands that are being made upon them, extremely difficult. It is not surprising, therefore, that HMI believed that departments were isolated from each other and may even be in direct competition, while teachers found it difficult to develop a collective and open approach to their professional activities.

The situation had changed a little by 1988 when HMI reported that:

In the best schools the head was supported by senior teachers who, well aware of their respective roles and responsibilities, were able to influence and involve the rest of the staff at appropriate levels of decision-making and action. But in many schools *the role of middle management, particularly that of heads of department, was under-developed.*

(DES 1988b: 6; my italics)

To some extent TVEI, profiling and similar initiatives have helped some schools to make progress towards a more collegial approach to their work. There is growing evidence of an increase in conscious planning and resource management that has been associated with such initiatives and to a more systematic and regular evaluation of work, often as part of more explicit management policies. HMI (DES 1988b) pointed to the growing importance of in-service training in management development, although they were concerned about the lack of coherent policies for staff induction and development in some schools.

These issues will all be dealt with in this book. They will be placed in the context of developing a team-based approach to all aspects of the management of secondary schools. This helps to ensure that the professional isolation of teachers in their different disciplines and areas can be overcome and enables schools to respond effectively to the challenges that they now face. The approach to school management taken here is derived from the basic premise that it should be based on teacher collaboration and professional expertise. Management in secondary schools should not be seen as:

> a set of techniques to be applied by a manager (the head or senior staff) to the managed (subordinate teachers or pupils) in order to regulate change in a direction considered to be appropriate by the senior staff.
>
> (Campbell 1985: 109)

The extent to which teachers recognise the centrality of management activities to the achievement of their educational objectives depends on the organisation of their particular school. The willingness of teachers to become involved in the management of their school depends on their understanding of the nature of management and its relevance to work in the classroom. With this in mind two questions take on a great significance. These are:

- What does management mean within the broad context of secondary education?
- How may management practices be identified and understood within secondary schools?

These questions raise complex issues that have to be addressed if individual teachers are to play an effective role in the management of their schools and if teachers within those schools are to be managed in such a way as to enable them to maximise their professional potential. To begin to examine these issues it is first necessary to look at the tasks which face managers at all levels in secondary schools.

THE TASKS OF MANAGEMENT IN SECONDARY SCHOOLS

Drucker (1968) drew attention to the complexities of management when he divided the tasks that face any manager into two specific parts:

> The manager has the task of creating a true whole that is larger than the sum of the parts, a productive entity that turns out more than the sum of the resources put into it . . . . The second specific task of the manager is to harmonize in every decision and action the requirements of immediate and long-range future. He cannot sacrifice either without endangering the

enterprise . . . . He must, so to speak, keep his nose to the grindstone while lifting his eyes to the hills.

(Drucker 1968: 408–9)

The picture which emerges if we try to visualise, for example, heads of department keeping their noses to the grindstone while lifting their eyes to the hills encapsulates many of the difficulties that face managers in secondary schools as they enter the last decade of the twentieth century. Dealing with the increasingly demanding day-to-day tasks of running the departmental team takes considerable time and effort. Planning for the future as it is shaped by the National Curriculum and new forms of school administration, management and accountability adds a further range of demands and responsibilities to those already facing the middle manager in the secondary school. Much the same can be said of those in other management positions. In order to cope with this situation priorities have to be identified and clear lines of communication allied to effective delegation and ways of sharing responsibilities established. There is need, therefore, to establish a clear understanding of those tasks to which Drucker refers.

As part of their work on staff selection in secondary schools Morgan *et al.* (1983) have suggested that those tasks which commonly face managers in a school setting can be subsumed under four headings:

(a) Technical: those tasks which are specific to the main purpose of the school, that is the education of its pupils. These will be concerned with the processes of teaching and learning.
(b) Conceptual: those tasks concerning the control and administration of the school such as the deployment of staff and the management of resources.
(c) Human relations: those tasks which are related to the structuring of participation in decision-making and policy-making and to staff development.
(d) External relations: those tasks which enable managers to control the flow of information into and out of the school and to manage the legitimate interventions in the life of the school from parents, governors and others within the community.

Central to the technical management tasks in any school is the management of the curriculum, not least because the curriculum and its assessment have been and will continue to be subject to significant changes that require skilful management. Such changes are, as Field reminds us:

the proper concern of staff, parents, pupils, governors and the LEA so that the time required for discussion and dissemination of information may be considerable.

(Field 1985: 309)

Governors are now required, under the terms of the 1988 Education Reform

Act to ensure that the National Curriculum is followed in their school and must produce a statement of aims for their school as well as specific statements about whether and how sex education should be included in the school curriculum. Hence they have an even more central role to play in the management of the school curriculum. Both managerial and educational considerations are involved in this process. Governors may be able to explore the former. The latter must be dealt with, at least in part, by those responsible for particular parts of the curriculum as well as the senior managers who have overall responsibility for curriculum provision within the school. Allied to this is the need to enable governors to manage the curriculum in a way which retains the existing good practice within the school.

A second major technical task in secondary schools is the provision of pastoral care. Structures for providing pastoral care and enabling schools to respond to the non-academic needs of pupils have grown and changed dramatically in recent years (see Best *et al.* 1980; Bell and Maher 1986). However, as many schools have become smaller through the decline in pupil numbers and as a greater emphasis has been placed on curricular rather than pastoral provision through the demands of the National Curriculum, the task of managing pastoral provision has become more demanding. The need to compete for scarce resources within the school at a time of extensive and rapid change has made the pastoral team leader's task even more difficult.

At the same time carrying out the conceptual tasks in schools has also become more demanding. Staff selection and deployment have always been part of the work required to manage any school but, as we saw in chapter 1, appointing staff with the relevant skills has in some areas become more difficult. With the implementation of the Education Act (DES 1986a) and the ERA (DES 1988a) governors now have a more direct role to play in staff appointments and, should it arise, in staff disciplinary procedures including those relating to dismissal. With the introduction of local management of schools the appointment, deployment and dismissal of staff have been devolved to schools in entirety provided that they operate within the legislation that controls such activities.

In order to manage staff even more effectively many schools have attempted to identify satisfactory indicators of staff and school performance which have led to the introduction of staff appraisals and performance reviews. This again consumes resources although it can also provide opportunities and benefits for individual members of staff as well as for the school as a whole. School development plans have to take into account the needs of individuals and groups, as well as of the whole school. Producing such plans forms a major part of the background against which have to be seen the conceptual tasks of the manager in the secondary school, the allocation of resources, and responsibility for buildings and resources.

Closely related to the conceptual management tasks in the school are the human relations tasks. These also have to be placed in the overall context of a school development plan. It is a basic theme of this book that effective school management requires a structure that enables staff to participate in the making of policy and the taking of decisions that affect their working lives. Many secondary schools are, by their very nature, hierarchical. This need not preclude staff co-operation and involvement in decision-making. It can be entirely appropriate for decisions to be devolved to a team or a department. Comments from such groups can and should be taken into account as part of the policy-making process that goes on in every school. Such involvement provides significant opportunities for enhancing the professional development of colleagues. Staff development is one of the major management responsibilities in all schools and it will be considered in detail in chapter 6.

The external management tasks, until recently, have tended to be regarded mainly as the province of the headteacher, except where pastoral work spills over to the home and community. This has been especially true in relation to governing bodies. It has been the headteacher who represented, some may say personified, the school to the outside world and who, in conjunction with the senior management team, mediated between the outside world and the school community. It was the head teacher who interpreted central and local government policy to colleagues inside the school and who gave the lead in any necessary policy-making in order to respond to such policy. It was the headteacher who tended to represent the school at governors' meetings, parents' evenings and at external events.

While the headteacher still remains the focal point of much of this type of activity many other staff are now increasingly involved in it. TVEI and similar developments have brought many teachers into contact with local industry and with steering groups on which can be found representatives of LEAs, industry, commerce, parents and community interests. Teachers are increasingly required to negotiate directly with examination boards, to work with colleagues from different schools to assess work produced by different groups of children and to co-operate in staff training and curriculum development. Reporting on children's progress to parents has usually formed a normal part of school life but reporting as envisaged by the National Curriculum will extend this activity and formalise the process. At the same time teachers are coming into more direct contact with governors as they assume a more central role in the management of schools.

In carrying out these wide-ranging tasks the role of senior and middle management is crucial, for good leadership by headteachers and heads of department is vital to the effectiveness of schools and to the quality of education that they provide (DES 1987c). Nevertheless, as Field (1985) has observed, it is extremely difficult to separate the technical (professional) from the executive (administrative) aspects of these tasks. Hughes *et al*.

(1985) have drawn attention to the importance of distinguishing between those tasks that a manager in a secondary school must carry out in providing professional leadership and those which relate to executive functions. The former include:

- providing professional guidance to staff;
- counselling pupils, parents and others;
- teaching and curriculum development;
- acting as spokesperson for the school on relevant educational matters;
- involvement in external professional activities.

The latter include:

- allocating resources and monitoring their use;
- co-ordinating functions within the school or department;
- establishing and maintaining external relationships with members of the governing body, the LEA and other organisations such as employers.

We will return to this division of function in chapter 3. For the moment it is worth noting that both the professional leadership and the executive functions apply to middle as well as senior managers. Both functions have an internal and an external dimension. Furthermore, identifying and managing this boundary between professional and administrative work will be a significant part of the managerial role played by senior managers in secondary schools in the future.

In order to manage this boundary, the tasks which face teachers with management responsibility in secondary schools have to be clearly understood. These can be subsumed under three deceptively simple headings:

(a) keeping things going: *administration* of the school and organising its routine activities;
(b) doing new things: *innovation* and bringing about necessary and planned changes;
(c) reacting to crisis: dealing with the unexpected and solving problems, often referred to as *salvation.*

Effective management demands that an appropriate balance is achieved between these three tasks. If any one set of tasks receives too much or too little consideration, the total work of the team will suffer. It is likely that it will be the day-to-day administration which saps the energy and imagination rather than the more demanding tasks on which colleagues might be engaged. These tasks and the everyday but unpredictable minor crises that litter our lives in schools seem to demand, and therefore receive, more immediate responses. Hence longer-term concerns and forward planning may be ignored. Our noses are sharpened on the grindstone of immediacy but our eyes are rarely, if ever, lifted towards the distant horizon.

AIMS AND SCHOOL MANAGEMENT

In order to reach these distant horizons the manager of the secondary school team will need, according to Everard and Morris (1985), a sense of purpose or mission. This should be derived directly from the cultural ethos of a school. It should be embedded in the reason for the existence of any school, that is to promote learning for its pupils within an appropriate curriculum. This will need to be located within an organisational structure that takes into account the tensions which may arise between teachers as autonomous professionals and teachers in their role as managers. Increasing the room for teachers to make professional judgements appears to be constrained by factors outside their immediate control.

The curriculum, the assessment of children's progress and the methods adopted for reporting that progress to parents and pupils all seem to be subject to direction from outside the immediate confines of the school. It is important, therefore, that any statement of mission or aims is derived from what the school actually does and is not a pious statement of what the school would like to do but will not be able to achieve. It is important to ensure that, wherever possible, staff are able to participate in the writing of such an aims statement in order that it has meaning for them and can be useful to them. Educational aims only provide an effective framework for a school if the staff have been involved in their construction. Without such an involvement there is a real danger that teachers will see the statement of aims as nothing more than the headteacher's view of the school. Ensuring that staff are involved is a task for managers at all levels in the school. It is especially true of senior managers who always have to remember that they are both leading professionals and senior managers. This means that they have to strike a balance. A balance between the educational good of the many and the short-term advantage of the few and between educational principles and philosophies and pragmatic necessity, especially in translating externally imposed priorities into school-based policies. Such judgements have to be made on the basis of a recognition that only certain things are possible at any one time and that where choices are to be made this must be done in terms of the educational aims which the school has established for itself.

Various groups have an interest in this process and can be described as stakeholders in what the school is doing. The pupils are stakeholders in this process because they have a vested interest in its outcomes. The same is true of their parents and teachers. At the same time the ERA emphasises that the Government has a stake in ensuring that policies are in place that will meet the needs of society and that LEAs have a role to play in ensuring that statutory requirements are met and that the system is managed efficiently. Potential employers and other groups in the community also have a stake in schools. The existence of such a wide range of stakeholders does not guarantee that their views will be in accord, nor that each set of views can be given equal value, especially where the boundaries between professional and non-professional areas are uncertain. In fact the reverse is probably true. The extent to which these tensions can be managed will depend on how clear those within the school are about what they are trying to do.

In the light of this, therefore, it can be seen that the prime task of management in the secondary school is to establish what the school's aim or mission statement is. The ERA gives some help here when it points out that:

the curriculum should be balanced and broadly based, and should:
(a) promote the spiritual, moral, cultural, mental and physical development of pupils at the school and of society; and
(b) prepare such pupils for the opportunities, responsibilities and experiences of adult life.

(DES 1988a: 7)

This statement reflects a concern with the needs of society at large as well as with outcomes of the teaching and learning processes that go on inside the school. It rests on the view that schools have as their special task to help children to mature and prepare themselves for adult responsibilities. These concerns need to be reflected in the statement of aims of each school. This is not an easy task and it must involve more than the identification of a wide range of objectives that each school ought to have. It has been suggested that one approach to producing a clear, useful statement of aims can be achieved if five basic steps are followed (Reed and Hall 1989). These are:

(a) Think of the school as a total process in which all the separate activities contribute to one whole. This whole, the school itself, is made distinct from other parts of the community by its boundaries.
(b) Clarify what you are trying to do when you are producing a statement of aims. You are not producing a summary of the aspirations of all or some of those inside the school, nor a description of what it already does. You are trying to state what the school is intending to achieve and the starting point for this is to look at what the school actually does achieve for its pupils by the time they leave.
(c) Construct a model of what goes on inside the school to help you in this process. Look at what comes into the school and what those inside the school have to work with. This will include children in the role of pupils and adults in various roles. It will also include resources, policies, needs and expectations, and buildings. There will also be inputs that are of special relevance to your particular school such as knowledge and experience of other cultures, specific resources and opportunities that exist within the community.
    Look then at what the school produces with its inputs – at what its outcomes are. These will include pupils with skills and abilities, teachers with a range of experiences, but it might also include some form of

community involvement or other specially relevant outcome. Note, however, that it is unwise to assume that pupils are passive recipients in this process for they play a significant part in determining its various outcomes.

Consider how these outcomes have been achieved, what the school does, in reality, to produce them. Forms of learning and teaching will be included here as will school administration, organisation and management and use of resources. Look at the unplanned activities and events as well as those that have been planned.

(d) Focus on the activities of the school to help define its aim. This is best done in small teams rather than with the whole staff. List all the processes that go on in the school and prioritise them to reflect the essential features of the school and its crucial functions. This listing of essential features and functions then needs to be carried out at the whole school level by the headteacher and the senior management team to combine the views expressed by other teams within the school and to give a school-based priority to what emerges. These views should not be forgotten, however, because each team within the school needs to have its own statement of aims that reflects the statement of aims of the whole school and guides the work of that particular team.

Once the listing of the essential features and functions has been done the statement of aims can be written. This should include a brief description of what the school is going to achieve in terms of the average successful pupil leaving that school. The statement, because it is brief, may exclude some important elements but all essential elements will be there.

(e) Check and test the statement of aims. The statement must be generally acceptable to governors, staff and others with a stake in the school. This must be checked. If it is to be of any value the statement must be useful. How far can it help governors and senior managers to make decisions about, for example, resource allocation within the school? Can pupils understand it? Does it provide guidance about the curriculum?

Remember that the statement of aims is not a once-and-for-all summary of what the school is trying to do. It will need constant revision as the world outside changes and as the school itself changes. This revision can start by looking at its relevance to teams within the school on a regular basis.

The importance of a statement of aims has been recognised in the ERA and its related Circular 14/89 (DES 1989c), which states in section 4A that as from January 1990 all county, controlled or maintained schools should provide a statement about the aims of the secular curriculum for parents. The importance of such statements of aims has also been recognised by HMI, which pointed out that the most effective schools:

had clear aims and associated objectives . . . set out in written statements of aims which were available to staff, pupils, parents and governors. Often, the production of written statements had been the result of extensive discussion and hence represented a commitment to beliefs collectively underwritten . . . . Moreover these aims were not left at the level of generalisation, but were translated into more precisely focused and specific objectives concerning the curriculum and pastoral care of all pupils. These objectives, in turn, became guidelines for action through, for example, departmental schemes of work and policies on matters such as marking, homework and discipline.

(DES 1988b: paras 2.1–2.19)

HMI went on to point out that effective schools had other characteristics in common. They were staffed by well qualified teachers with a good blend of experience and expertise who were provided with opportunities for their own professional development within the overall context of the needs of the school. The staff planned and implemented a coherent curriculum within which due attention was given to cross-curricular aspects. Means were set up to identify and develop all pupils' particular strengths and to offer appropriate challenges. Lessons took place in an atmosphere which was relaxed and orderly and where positive encouragement was given to pupils. This concern for pupils was reflected in the pastoral care arrangements that each school made, based on a detailed knowledge of each pupil's individual performance.

The most effective schools also had the capacity to cope with and to manage change, to solve problems, and to develop organically rather than seeking to remain static in a changing environment. Responsiveness, adaptability and the ability to plan and initiate strategies for whole school development were significant features of these schools. They brought together human and material resources, curriculum planning and teaching and learning to cater for the needs of pupils. Above all, they were well managed and well led. In this the role of the headteacher was of crucial importance. The capacity to enthuse and support others in order to achieve objectives and the ability to delegate effectively to teams and individuals were essential features of the most skilful headteachers. These qualities were also in evidence at various levels within the school, so that managing the effective school could be seen as a team effort between supportive professional colleagues. Thus middle managers, such as heads of departments and heads of year, have a central part to play in the running of the school. They cannot play a full part in this if their perspective is limited to their department or pastoral team and does not encompass the whole school context. Middle managers must work both within their teams and outside their teams in order to make the most effective contribution to the school.

We can see, therefore, that school management is about creating a framework for effective teaching and learning. It is about flexibility and being accountable. One of the central tasks of school management is the deployment of resources in pursuit of the aims of the school. A school's effectiveness has to be judged by how far it proves to be able to achieve its aims and to meet its objectives. This may be a matter for professional judgement rather than a set of performance indicators. Where you have a widely accepted statement of aims that is understood by teachers, governors, pupils and parents, then such a judgement about the effectiveness of a school is likely to be realistic and supportive. How then, can school effectiveness be achieved?

WHAT IS SCHOOL EFFECTIVENESS?

School effectiveness means getting things done through other people and supporting them in all that they need to do in order to establish and sustain their effectiveness. Effective team leadership, therefore, is vital to the management of every school. It has been suggested, however, that effectiveness is extremely difficult to define in an educational context (Reid *et al.* 1987). In the previous section we saw how effectiveness was defined in the context of the National Curriculum. The main elements of that definition were that an effective school would: maximise pupil achievement; care for the development of the whole individual; and prepare pupils for adult life.

On the other hand Reid *et al.* (1987) suggest that any such definition of effectiveness will tend to limit the educational horizons of schools and that, in any case, any attempt to define effectiveness will be based on value judgements. They go on to argue that their perspective is that an effective school will value certain factors such as:

- the improvement of both teaching and learning;
- the development of the school as a learning institution;
- the humanisation of schooling;
- the total involvement of staff in both collaboration and democratic collegiality;
- an awareness of the benefits of both process and product;
- the research-based, INSET-based nature of school development.

It could be argued that effective schools develop effectively – and they develop effectively by examining both the normative and procedural dimensions. This leads to the drawing of a vital distinction between a 'good' and an 'effective' school. The latter develops successfully in *any* direction; the former develops successfully according to an agreed . . . agenda.

(Reid *et al.* 1987: 12)

It is difficult to know just how valid this distinction is between good and effective, in the present climate where much of the agenda is predetermined for most schools. It is clear, however, that effectiveness is concerned with achieving agreed objectives whether or not these objectives are selected from a broad, *à la carte* menu of choices or from a more restricted *table d'hôte* of options. A school, therefore, is effective insofar as it accomplishes what it sets out to do. Effectiveness is not an all-or-nothing proposition; a school may be only partially effective.

The same is equally true for the teams that go to make up the school. The point to notice here, however, is that effectiveness is defined in terms of the school's or the team's own expectations. It follows, then, that care has to be taken to ensure that these expectations are in accord with the expectations of all the stakeholders in the school and are appropriately located within the overall aims of the school itself. For this reason alone staff should have the school's statement of aims constantly in mind and should play an active part in its construction. At the same time middle managers need to recognise that what they and their team do makes a crucial contribution to the overall work of the whole school. The work of the team should not be viewed in isolation. It is essential that team leaders pay some attention to what their objectives are and how they can best be achieved within the wider framework of each particular school. Managing teams in schools is an essential part of managing for effectiveness. How then, can we manage for effectiveness?

MANAGING FOR SCHOOL EFFECTIVENESS

Managing for effectiveness has to take place, according to Peters and Waterman (1982), within a flexible organisational structure which is not rooted in the assumption that anyone moving into a position in an organisation will behave in exactly the same way as his or her predecessor. This view is based on a major study of seventy-five highly regarded companies in the USA. They discovered that 'the excellent companies were, above all, brilliant on the basics' (Peters and Waterman 1982: 13). They argued that eight similar characteristics were found in all of the most effective companies. Handy (1984) has related these criteria to schools. The Peters and Waterman criteria are:

(a) A bias for action, for getting on with it. Formal procedures are not allowed to stultify decision-making and action. Effective schools will be geared to action and the people within them will look for opportunities to get things done.
(b) Getting close to the customer and learning from the people they serve. The school has to know what is expected of it by its stakeholders and be committed to the children and their learning above all else.
(c) Autonomy and entrepreneurship is encouraged. Experimentation and risk-taking will be encouraged at all levels in the school. Failure is seen as part of learning for all, not as something to be condemned.

(d) Productivity through people inside the organisation. Everybody within the school is regarded as a source of ideas and the contribution of each is valued. This is allied to clear and high expectations of both staff and pupils.

(e) A hands-on, value-driven philosophy. The basic philosophy of the school must be clear to all. Everyone in the school must support these values and use them as a basis for decision-making.

(f) Stick to the knitting and do what you know. Effective schools keep to what they do best and use this to guide decision-making especially in the area of staff appointment and development.

(g) Simple form, lean staff with a flexible structure. Schools should aim for as simple a management structure as possible and minimise complexity and bureaucratic patterns of organisation.

(h) Simultaneous loose–tight properties. Effective schools have a well established and firm central control but with a high degree of autonomy for individuals and groups within the school.

There are some contextual difficulties in applying to the world of education such a list of attributes derived from the world of American business. It is difficult, for example, to specify in relatively simple terms what the product of education might be. Educational performance is not easily measurable in terms of profit and loss or even in terms of cost per pupil. Nevertheless the list draws our attention to the vital importance of being clear about what we are trying to do and how we intend to set about doing it. It also emphasises the importance of giving responsibilities to teachers, of valuing teachers for what they do and of encouraging, helping and supporting them in being even more effective.

There are interesting similarities between the characteristics identified by Peters and Waterman (1982) and those emphasised by HMI on the basis of their observations of good practice in schools. They show that:

> The value of clear objectives for each lesson, and the need for pupils to understand these objectives are often demonstrated. . . . References to the importance of professional team work occur frequently in school reports. . . . The survey recorded the influence on the quality of work exerted by teachers with delegated responsibilities who were 'involving colleagues in cooperative planning by working alongside teachers in the classroom, by identifying needs for in-service training and, in particular, by demonstrating through personal example what could be achieved'. These comments emphasise the importance of professional team work for maximum curricular strength and support.
>
> (DES 1985b: paras. 13–30)

These characteristics, which exemplify a range of good practice in schools, are similar to those lists derived from industry and commerce. Such a list would include:

- setting clear objectives and ensuring that they were understood by colleagues and pupils;
- planning with colleagues to ensure a unity of purpose;
- establishing a consistency of approach but enabling each to contribute as effectively as possible;
- providing leadership through example, support and effective teamwork;
- giving guidance in a range of professional matters and encouraging innovation;
- assessing performance of children and taking responsibility for the work of colleagues in relevant areas;
- co-operating as a team in order to provide a framework within which each individual can work effectively;
- developing colleagues and recognising the value of each individual contribution.

These characteristics are not merely descriptions of existing practice in those schools that have recently benefited from a general inspection and which may be thought of as good or effective schools. They form an extensive working definition of what constitutes good professional practice in schools. In many of our more effective secondary schools such characteristics will be found as a normal and well developed part of school life. Other schools are at the point of developing their own individual responses to expectations such as these, while some schools may not yet have crossed that particular threshold. It is clear, however, whatever its stage of development, the responsibility for managing the school devolves to the whole staff of that school as individuals and as members of the different working groups that go to make up the organisation of that school.

ACTIVITIES

1 Examine how the four tasks of management identified by Morgan, Hall and Mackay (1983) are carried out in your school.
2 Look at the statement of aims of your school. How can you use it to inform what you do in school? How far can the five-stage process recommended by Reed and Hall (1989) be used to produce a statement of aims for your team?
3 See how far you can apply the Peters and Waterman (1982) criteria for managing for effectiveness to your school or to your team.

Chapter 3

Leadership and management in secondary schools

Any discussion of management skills within any context will soon highlight two basic issues. These are: 'What is to be managed?' which focuses attention on the essential nature of the organisation and upon its fundamental purposes, and 'How shall it be managed?' which raises questions about the type of skills and abilities which may be useful, desirable, applicable or necessary in the particular circumstances. The issues raised by these two questions are closely interconnected and may be difficult to separate in the daily turmoil of school life. Nevertheless, it might be useful here to consider them as discrete questions in order to highlight our concern with the need for all managers in secondary schools to acquire and develop those skills which might enable them to establish and sustain effective teams of teachers in their schools. The first of the two basic issues, addressed in the previous chapter, refers to the various technical, conceptual, human relations and external relations tasks that have to be managed in schools.

It has been suggested (Day *et al.* 1985), with particular reference to the professional development of teachers, that there are a number of tasks that are the legitimate concern of every leader of every team of teachers in every school:

(a) the school's climate: this is the embodiment of a range of policies about how the various groups and individuals within the school work together;
(b) the curriculum and the related teaching and learning processes: these represent those aspects of knowledge and skill that the school regards as important, and the significant ways of transmitting those skills and knowledge areas;
(c) the management of relationships within the school: ways of organising staff teams to ensure a unity of purpose within the team and between different teams within the school;
(d) involvement in the processes of evaluating, assessing and recording the work of their pupils as well as their own performance.

Implicit here is the assumption that, if people are involved in managing the processes that shape their activities, then they are likely to be more committed to their work. This is often referred to as collegial authority, the main features of which are that:

- teachers integrate their work on a team basis;
- teams have an internal democracy;
- teams determine their objectives in the light of school goals and the key objectives as set out in the school development plan;
- school goals are determined by a process that involves all staff;
- evaluation of teacher performance will be by fellow professionals;
- support in the form of staff development will be available to all staff.

(adapted from Hoyle 1986: 87)

It is on such a foundation that successful teamwork in secondary schools can be built. It should be recognised, however, that there are significant barriers to such collegiality (Hoyle 1986): the extent to which authority within the school is vested in the governors and delegated to the headteacher; the related requirement that the school, through the headteacher, should be accountable to its stakeholders. Collegial authority of this kind may also result in a closer control over what teachers do and how they do it. This trend is accentuated by some aspects of the National Curriculum. If teachers are to work together the need to meet together on a regular basis will increase, as will the need to produce documents for such meetings and as a result of such meetings. Some of this work may be encompassed within directed time in many schools. The use of time can be enhanced by organising meetings even more effectively. This consideration of collegiality brings us to the second of the questions which were posed in the opening paragraph of this chapter.

HOW IS THE SCHOOL MANAGED?

The work of all teachers and the teams to which they belong is carried out within a framework that is partly created by the arrangements that have been made for governing the school. The governing body is responsible for: the general conduct of the school including making decisions about the appropriate curriculum; in the light of LEA policies deciding whether or not to include sex education; providing general principles to be followed in formulating a policy on discipline; controlling the resources of the school and, in particular, managing the finances of the school; appointing, promoting, redeploying and dismissing staff; admission arrangements for pupils, including setting the physical capacity for the school; and reporting annually to parents of pupils at the school. At the same time as these new powers came into operation the composition of governing bodies changed to increase the representation of parents and members of the local community.

These changes have altered the ways in which most governing bodies operate and have led to a restructuring of relationships between governors and school staff. It is already clear that, at the very least, most governing bodies are now having to meet more than once a term, the norm before September 1989. Many governing bodies have established a series of sub-committees or working parties to deal with particular areas of responsibility. As a result, the reporting arrangements on governing bodies need to be reconsidered. The termly report from the headteacher may already contain sufficient information to enable many such sub-committees to function effectively, but in the case of the groups responsible for finance and staffing matters in particular, much more information may well be needed. The nature and pattern of reports to governors may need to change. Much more information will be available in the form of financial statements from the LEA. The headteacher will find it difficult to represent the school on all these groups even if that were appropriate. In many schools deputy heads and, for curriculum and resourcing matters, department heads, are playing a more active role in establishing relationships with governors. It should be recognised that the headteacher has the prime responsibility for representing the school on the governing body even on detailed curriculum matters. The headteacher retains the overall responsibility for the internal management of the school, but has to ensure that colleagues can play a significant part in that process.

CHANGING MANAGEMENT ROLES IN SCHOOLS

A recent study involving a sample of 630 headteachers has shown that over two-thirds of secondary and almost four-fifths of primary headteachers regarded the move away from headteacher to manager or chief executive as the most significant change in their role (NFER 1989). A few headteachers welcomed this change but most were concerned about the increasing volume of work and its changing nature. They pointed out that boundary management, including public relations and marketing, was becoming an ever more significant part of their role and that demands related to accountability featured more prominently than had been the case in the past. At the same time a tremendous increase in head teachers' work in relation to the governing body was also identified especially in areas directly related to the internal management of the school.

Managing the internal functioning of the school and its boundary are not new responsibilities for headteachers. In 1977 it was recognised in *Ten Good Schools* (DES 1977b) that the headteacher needed to be a good diplomat, a negotiator, a public relations officer and a personnel manager. These were not roles that were traditionally associated with headship at that time. What is missing is the external dimension that the current shift in educational policy is emphasising.

This missing element was recognised recently by a group of newly appointed headteachers in a Midlands' LEA who were asked to identify their expectations about the main roles that they would have to play as headteachers (Bell 1986). They listed five different roles within the overall context of having responsibility for the education and welfare of children.

- Teaching and providing professional leadership.
- Managing colleagues and helping to develop their expertise.
- Setting educational priorities for their schools.
- Building good working relationships inside school, including relationships with parents and governors.
- Basic administration.

When the same headteachers were asked to indicate how they saw their role changing as a result of the ERA they suggested that the emphasis on caring for children would give way to a concern for maintaining the system within which they worked. They listed five main functions.

- Testing and assessing children and colleagues.
- Directing and controlling the professional activities of teachers.
- Managing resources on the basis of priorities that were set elsewhere.
- Public relations to various audiences.
- Basic administration including assisting with the financial and resource management of the school.

While the position of headteacher has always had two basic dimensions – the educational or professional dimension and the managerial or executive dimension – the traditional view of the headteacher tended to emphasise the former, while recent developments are placing more emphasis on the latter. As Maclure has argued:

> The head has always had a powerful management role. . . . The new dispensation ushered in by the Education Reform Act puts this on a new basis. . . . The element of financial delegation ensures that this change will be real. . . . The head's enhanced management role cannot but change relationships within the profession as a whole.
>
> (Maclure 1989: 11–12)

Nowhere is this more true than in the headteacher's relationship with the deputy. It has long been recognised that the role of the deputy is one which is defined almost entirely by the headteacher. The deputy becomes what the headteacher allows (Matthew and Tong 1982). It has been suggested (Riches 1988) that 'deputy' is really a misnomer since few holders of the posts do, in fact, deputise. In any case, the role is much wider and more complicated than the term would seem to imply. The role may be defined formally in terms of a job description and informally through a wide range of expectations that come from the deputy head's role set. One study, based on an analysis of advertisements for deputy head posts, concluded that the picture which emerges of the ideal candidate is that of a person of considerable presence, self-confident and energetic, with administrative skills, able to timetable, work in teams, chair meetings, teach well and have a flair for public relations (Owen *et al.* 1983).

It comes as little surprise, therefore, to discover that deputy heads tend to have the least clearly defined job descriptions of any senior or middle management post in schools. It is an opportunity for some to be a head-in-waiting, but for many more it is the final post (Torrington and Weightman 1989a).

Where the deputy headship is the head-in-waiting stage it has been suggested (Lawley 1988) that there are a number of activities that ought to form part of the deputy's routine duties. These include:

- chairing meetings and working parties;
- being involved in the appointment of staff;
- attending governors' meetings;
- managing change;
- working with the community;
- working with HMI and LEA inspectors;
- involvement with industry.

Many of these ought to form, and will form, part of the job of deputy heads and may increasingly do so. Lawley (1988) has also gone one stage further by identifying six key tasks for deputies whether they are at the head-in-waiting stage or not. These are dealing with parents; industrial relations; sites and buildings; primary school liaison; working with HMI and LEA inspectors; and working with people inside the school.

Dealing with parents This involves working with individual parents and providing opportunities for groups of parents to encounter the school in various ways. Direct contact with individual parents often involves coping with and trying to solve problems related to pupils and demands a high degree of tact and diplomacy. Working with groups of parents often involves running meetings and giving information which requires planning and organisational skills.

Industrial relations Unions and professional associations have come to play a far more significant part in school life in recent years. As more powers and responsibilities are devolved to schools this trend will be accentuated. The school may become the main forum for bargaining about pay and conditions. Deputy heads have a major role to play in this process.

Sites and buildings Many schools were beginning to appoint bursars prior to the delegation of financial responsibilities. Now, with the possibility of entering into contracts for repairs, maintenance and minor building work as well as having a budget for such matters, more work related to sites and buildings will be devolved to the senior staff in schools, in conjunction with governing bodies.

Primary school liaison As pupil numbers have declined and competition for pupils has grown, liaising with feeder schools has become a vital part of the work of most secondary schools. The benefits of an effective and smooth transfer from one school to another accrue most to pupils; but teachers also gain from closer contact, a more efficient transfer of records and a growing understanding of what is done in other parts of the education system. This activity will, at times, extend into marketing the school.

Working with HMI and LEA inspectors As these groups take on a monitoring and evaluation role in respect of the National Curriculum it is likely that headteachers and deputies will be even more aware of the importance of maintaining contact with them and benefiting from their expertise.

Working with people inside the school At various times most deputy heads will be responsible for pupil welfare, probationary staff and staff development. Deputy heads, more than anyone else in the school, are often in a position to examine the impact of the curriculum as it is organised on individual groups of children (and teachers). This is well worth doing from time to time especially as education moves into a new phase of curriculum organisation which is driven by the need to implement the National Curriculum.

The tasks described are often carried out by deputy heads but they are not restricted to this group. Headteachers and middle managers have a part to play in all of these tasks. It does, however, seem to fall to deputy heads to carry the major burden for most of them, often acting for the headteacher.

It has been suggested, however, that the deputy who may once have been the headteacher's day-to-day executive functionary is now a part of the corporate management structure of the school. Nicholson (1989) welcomes this development arguing:

> It is essential that senior staff work as a team, complementing and supporting each other and sharing tasks. Structures which begin with 'Deputy Head – Academic' and 'Deputy Head – Pastoral' are likely to make existing staff divisions worse.
>
> (Nicholson, 1989: 75)

If the expectations of changes in the role of deputy heads that were identified in the NFER study materialise, then the old academic/pastoral division may soon be a thing of the past. This study (NFER 1989) drew attention to the extent to which deputies were being faced with increased responsibilities. As headteachers spend more time on managing the boundary, so the deputy heads can be expected to devote more time to the internal management of the school, including staff development and liaising with governing bodies. In some schools deputies were not just taking on more responsibility for professional leadership, they were also acquiring new roles and new responsibilities related to resource management and the management of sites and buildings. All this, however, needs to be placed in the context of a management team that is inclusive rather than exclusive and that functions well, ensuring that teachers and children are able to get on with the essential processes of teaching and learning. Increasingly a team that does not work together effectively will generate stress among its members and will be less effective as the pressure to manage changes increases.

Ensuring that teams work together is the responsibility of those teachers who occupy what have become known as middle management positions within secondary schools. This term has unfortunate industrial connotations but, since it is now in common usage, it will be used here. It will be used to refer to heads of faculty, department, house or year and also to those colleagues with a cross-curricular or major extra-curricular responsibility. Concern about the quality of heads of department and other middle managers in secondary schools is widespread (Nicholson 1989). As HMI has commented:

> The vital importance of the role of the head of department is that it lies at the heart of the educational process. . . . Whether a student achieves or underachieves is largely dependent on the quality of the planning, execution and evaluation that takes place within the individual departments. . . . Yet in the majority of schools the full potential of the role has not been developed.
>
> (HMI, Wales undated: 21, quoted in Preedy 1988: 118)

This may well be because the appropriate training and support has not, as yet, been provided for people in such positions who have tended to be appointed for their expertise as teachers rather than for their skills as managers. It may also be due to the very nature of the middle management role itself which is not always clearly defined, especially in very small departments. Ribbins (1988) shows that middle managers are often subjected to a range of different, even conflicting expectations. This can be illustrated by looking at a broad classification of the functions of a head of department. These fall into three parts: academic, representative and managerial.

Academic Those matters relating to the subject, its position within the curriculum, its teaching, including methodology, and the learning of pupils. This may involve belonging to cross-curricular groups within the school and to curriculum working parties or relevant professional bodies outside the school.

Representative Representing the subject to the school, to parents and pupils and representing the school to the department. It may also include representing the department to those outside the school such as inspectors and advisers.

Managerial The planning, organising, controlling and evaluating of all aspects of the work of the department and reporting on the same to the head or senior management team and, where appropriate, parents and governors. This includes the managing of staff, resources and communication.

We can see these duties elaborated and made more specific in *The Cockroft Report* (DES 1982) where the list of duties for which a head of a mathematics department should take responsibility is said to include:

- the production of schemes of work;
- the organising of the department and its teaching resources;
- the monitoring of teaching within the department;
- the monitoring of the work of pupils in the department;
- the professional development and in-service training of those who teach mathematics;
- liaising with other departments in the school;
- liaising with other schools and colleges.

Marland, summarising much of his extensive work on the functions of the middle manager in secondary schools, identifies ten tasks that may be expected of such teachers. These are to:

- structure a team;
- take part in appointing staff;
- deploy teachers . . . consistent with their strengths, weaknesses, career development and the needs of the school;
- monitor teachers' work;
- assist the development of teachers' professional skills;
- contribute to the initial training of teachers;
- take part in the planning of the school's overall curriculum and lead curriculum planning in the department;
- oversee the work of pupils;
- manage the finances, physical resources and learning methods efficiently;
- assist in the overall leadership of the school.

(Adapted from Marland and Hill 1981: 2)

We can see, therefore, that the middle manager's role has elements which are internal and external to the school. It is based upon subject knowledge and expertise and the capacity to provide leadership. It also includes resource management, monitoring and evaluation, and staff development. It involves ensuring that policies are agreed and implemented, records kept and performance reviewed. Much of the work of the middle manager is carried out through other people. Interpersonal skills are important here. If colleagues are to be involved fully then meetings have to be organised and run effectively. These must lead to decisions being made, communicated and implemented, changes being managed and progress checked. Above all the middle managers must be able to manage their personal time well. Thus, the middle management role, like that of the headteacher and deputy head, requires a high degree of managerial and leadership skills if it is to be carried out successfully. What, then, are these skills?

MANAGEMENT SKILLS IN SECONDARY SCHOOLS

Hughes *et al.* (1985) point us towards one set of skills when he reminds us that Fayol (1916) defined the basis of management as: forecasting, planning, organising, commanding, co-ordinating and controlling. This list, of course, is derived from industrial practice and does not take full account of those interactive elements which are essential features where all the parties have professional responsibilities and commitment. Drucker (1968) helps in this respect when he adds motivating, communicating with and developing people. He also includes setting objectives rather than forecasting as a prelude to planning. He warns, however, that managing effectively requires more from an individual than the ability to apply such skills to particular situations. As he points out, the characteristic which identifies the successful manager in any enterprise is an educational one:

> The one contribution he is uniquely expected to make is to give others vision and ability to perform. It is vision and moral responsibility that, in the last analysis, define the manager.

> (Drucker 1968: 418)

This is nowhere truer than in the case of somebody with management responsibility for a team of teachers. Each member of the team has a body of professional knowledge and expertise that can and should be employed for the benefit of the children in the school and which can also usefully be imparted to colleagues. Each member of the team can benefit from the expertise of the others yet within this framework the activities of the team have to be co-ordinated, decisions taken and implemented, tasks delegated, and their effectiveness monitored and evaluated.

If we now look towards educational rather than industrial sources for indications as to what skills can help in the management of teams of teachers we find that in *Good Teachers* (DES 1985b) it is suggested that teachers as managers need to be concerned with setting objectives, co-ordinating cross-curricular activity, helping with the work of colleagues and extending and improving their performance. The Education (School Teachers' Pay and

Conditions) Order (DES 1987a) adds performance appraisal, the management of resources and formal responsibility for staff development. We can now identify twelve management skills that are vital for those who manage teams in schools.

Planning This is the identification of a course of action in order to achieve desired results. These results will be expressed in terms of objectives and will be derived from the school development plan and the priorities that it identifies.

Decision-making In essence, decision-making means choosing from at least two possible courses of action. It is one of the central skills of management since most of us spend much of our time making such choices. Within the context of team management particular care has to be taken to involve colleagues in the decision-making process.

Organising Organising means ensuring that all members of the team are working together co-operatively and that all the necessary functions and tasks are being carried out.

Co-ordinating This is closely related to organising. Duties have to be defined and responsibilities allocated fairly if co-ordination is to be effective.

Commanding This often has unfortunate authoritarian overtones which are not acceptable among a group of professional colleagues. In the context of team management, however, commanding is the ability to give clear instructions and information where this is appropriate.

Controlling Again, the notion of control runs contrary to the ethos of professional autonomy. After the ERA it is clear, however, that control is necessary to ensure that the National Curriculum is provided, that resources are managed effectively and that schools are able to be accountable to the various stakeholders. Controlling is the monitoring of performance to ensure that objectives are being achieved and tasks completed.

Delegating Delegating takes place when work is divided up among colleagues. The tasks to be delegated should be clearly identified and the person to whom a task is being given should be adequately prepared and supported.

Motivating Motivating can be defined as the process of encouraging colleagues to work more enthusiastically. It involves making behavioural choices, decisions about objectives and assumptions about rewards.

Developing staff Staff development is now an integral part of school development and a responsibility of all managers in schools who have to ensure that colleagues within their teams are given the maximum opportunity to benefit from individual professional development as part of school development.

Communicating This is an essential management skill since decisions can only be made, plans implemented, activities co-ordinated and controlled, tasks delegated, staff motivated and developed through an effective system of communication. It is now part of our responsibility to communicate with stakeholders, especially parents and governors.

Monitoring Monitoring is the process of ensuring that appropriate actions are being taken at the right time, checking that control and co-ordination are working effectively.

Evaluating Evaluating is the process of examining performance against previously identified and agreed criteria to ensure that those criteria are being met.

All of these skills are interdependent. Planning requires evaluation and monitoring, organising requires delegation, and motivating is necessary to get most things done. Management, then, can best be understood as:

> a continuous process through which members of an organisation seek to coordinate their activities and utilise their resources in order to fulfil the various tasks of the organisation as efficiently as possible.
>
> (Hoyle 1981: 8)

In the context of teams of teachers in secondary schools, management is the application of a specific set of skills in order to establish a professional collaboration between colleagues to achieve a set of common objectives. With the introduction of school development plans, these objectives and the tasks which have to be completed in order to achieve them will be written down, known and understood by all concerned.

LEADERSHIP IN SCHOOL TEAMS

The relationship between management and leadership is a complex one since it is not always possible in a school to make a clear distinction between the communicating, co-ordinating, planning, evaluating and related activities of management and the emphasis on working with, supporting, developing and encouraging staff, which is the province of leadership.

Leadership is more than the simple application of management functions, many of which may have to do with administration and the maintenance of the school. Effective management requires successful leadership since, as we have seen in this and the two previous chapters, all schools are required increasingly to adapt to new circumstances rather than be able to rely on what has gone before. Therefore, the style of leadership employed by those whom Coulson (1977) identified as having ego identification with the school is no longer appropriate. Such identification resulted in them regarding the school as their own property towards which they and they alone exercised a deep sense of responsibility for everyone in it and everything which happened within it. Such people may or may not have been born leaders. They would certainly have claimed the right to leadership through their status position in their schools. Such a form of leadership tends to become ascribed rather than achieved, in that its main features seem to be vested in one powerful individual within the school. It is verging on what Paisey (1984) has called congenital leadership: that is, leaders who are born rather than fashioned by environment. He also identifies situational leadership which, he argues, focuses on the relative nature of leadership and the extent to which opportunities for leadership are created by specific situations; and management leadership which he suggests is leadership based on holding a particular office such as headteacher.

Embodied in this definition of leadership are two related concerns: for the tasks of the organisation and for people. People in leadership positions will differ in the extent to which they emphasise each of these concerns. Nias suggests that an effective leader in a school will:

- set a high professional standard;
- have a high level of personal involvement in the school;
- be readily available, especially for discussion;
- be interested in individual teacher development;
- give a lead in establishing aims for the school;
- encourage participation in goal-setting and decision-making.

(after Nias 1980: 260)

This broad description of the elements of a leadership style still leaves significant scope for different forms of actual behaviour even within the framework of positive leadership. In any given circumstances a leader might:

- assert her own centrality by taking and announcing decisions;
- involve the group by explaining decisions;
- give the group power by encouraging it to select from a range of options;
- develop group power by encouraging it to suggest solutions;
- submit to group power by devolving decision-making to the group on certain issues within identified parameters;
- act as one of the group where the group defines its own authority over particular issues.

(derived from Tannenbaum and Schmidt 1958)

A number of factors may influence the choices which a leader makes; the extent to which she feels it is appropriate that her colleagues ought to be involved in the particular decision; her own self-confidence and her confidence in her colleagues; and her personal inclinations, since some people feel happier when working as members of a group, while others feel more comfortable taking responsibility alone. All of these factors will influence how a leader chooses to lead. Her judgement might also be affected by her colleagues. For example, she may know that her colleagues prefer to be involved in taking certain decisions or even that they expect to be included in the taking of some decisions. A wise leader will not ignore this. Similarly her colleagues may have significant relevant expertise which demands that they should be involved in some aspect of the school's work.

The leader may also be influenced by the specific situation. If it requires a rapid response then involving colleagues may prove difficult. If it requires detailed specialist knowledge then certain colleagues may need to be involved but not others. A decision may have a far-reaching impact on the work of some members of the staff. Perhaps they should be involved in the discussions about that decision even if they do not help to make the final choice or determine the preferred solution.

Leadership style, then, is a product of the interaction between a number of factors. Concern for defining and achieving tasks, concern for the interpersonal relationships within the group, choices about appropriate methods of involving colleagues in the work of the group are all part of leadership behaviour. Adair (1983) in his work on effective leadership, subsumes these points under the headings of:

- achieving the task;
- building and maintaining the staff team.

His third element of leadership behaviour is one concerned with:

- developing each individual.

He expresses these in terms of three overlapping circles which indicate that any single element of leadership behaviour can and will combine with any other single element, but that leadership within any group will only be really effective if all three elements receive sufficient attention. For example, the failure to build the team successfully in a school can easily result in failure to achieve those tasks which have been identified as important to that school. Similarly, if the development of individuals is entirely sacrificed for the building of a team and the achievement of its tasks, then individual members may soon become disillusioned and demotivated. As a result tasks will not be achieved and the team will cease to be effective.

Thus, it can be argued that the key elements in leadership are the integration of individual, team and school goals. It is clear that this approach requires the leader to understand what motivates her colleagues. She also has to be able to help the team to identify and achieve its goals. She may, as schools become more collegial, need to operate through processes of consultation and participation. She will need to maximise the individual's opportunities as well as her responsibilities for the attainment of the team's goals. Such an approach to leadership requires that team leaders see their team members as professional colleagues or, at the very least, seek to develop situations in which they can respond as professional colleagues.

MANAGING AND LEADING PROFESSIONAL TEACHERS

Most teachers working in schools regard themselves, and wish to be regarded by others, as professionals. This has implications for the ways in which schools are managed and for the ways in which groups of teachers work together with leaders. Handy (1984) has suggested that in organisations such as schools which are staffed by professionals, the professionals like to manage themselves. Indeed our commonly accepted notion of the meaning of professionalism contains the idea of autonomous groups which exercise control over their own actions on behalf of others, normally their clients. Writers such as Leiberman (1956), Millerson (1964) and Hoyle (1974) have identified a number of characteristics which might be used to identify a profession. These include:

- a body of knowledge on which practices are based;
- a lengthy period of training during which knowledge and skills are acquired;
- a concern with the welfare of the client;
- a high degree of autonomy;
- a code of ethics governing professional relationships.

How far those occupational groups which are generally regarded as professions actually exhibit any or all of these characteristics is not particularly significant in the context of our discussion of managing professionals in the school. What is important is the extent to which such characteristics shape the expectations of teachers, governors, parents and pupils within the school. It is clear that teachers undergo training and, in many cases, in-service training. They have a commitment to their pupils and they expect to retain a high degree of control over what they do in their classrooms based on this training and this commitment. Such claims to professional autonomy have been described as 'a new despotism' (Musgrove and Taylor 1969).

It has even been argued that because professionals are self-directed they do not need to be managed. This position is based on the view that either all decisions are group decisions or, alternatively, any decision taken by one professional will be very much like that taken by another (Rust 1985). This is an extremely simplistic view of professionalism and professionals. Few, if any schools, even those staffed by the most highly committed and sophisticated professional teachers, are likely to exhibit such unity and accord on all matters. Furthermore, teachers are often struggling to cope with the pedagogic demands which are made upon them and may not always have the time to devote to management activities even in the most collegial of schools. Thus, management of professional people and leadership of professional groups is vitally necessary. Management and leadership tend to mediate between the needs and expectations of the teachers, those of their pupils, and those identified as part of the school within which they work. It is the function of the managers in the school and the leaders of groups of teachers to help to break down the physical and social separation which results from the way in which much of a teacher's work is structured. A well-managed school is one in which professional colleagues share the responsibilities associated with the work of the school. Different individuals take the lead in different areas of school life, depending on their expertise. Such an approach to management can go a long way towards minimising the professional isolation that some school teachers experience.

Professional autonomy is not readily compatible with collegiality which requires a commitment to sharing expertise and to benefiting from the expertise of others. Those teachers who work in situations where teams of teachers share expertise within the framework of a well-structured school organisation are not likely to be professionally independent. They are more likely to exhibit professional interdependence. This requires that they are treated as professionals by the headteacher and by senior colleagues. It also requires that they act as professionals who have a concern for the whole school rather than for their own classroom alone. Professional teachers have to be managed in such a way as to recognise their claims to professional status. Such claims must not be allowed to prevent the development of whole-school policies which are founded on interdependence within a group of professional colleagues. Headteachers, deputy heads, team leaders and teachers with other responsibilities all have to understand the importance of professional interdependence and how to achieve it. This requires a knowledge of those specific skills which form the broad definition of management. It also requires the ability to apply those skills in order to achieve the tasks of the group, whether the group be the whole school or a small part of it. Task achievement has to be done at the same time as team building and the development of individuals within the team. In this way the management and leadership of a group of professional colleagues can begin to be effective.

Much depends, however, on the expectations which individuals have when they enter the school. For teachers this normally means when they were appointed. Selection and appointment procedures are, in many cases, the starting point of creating an ethos within which groups of teachers can co-operate as a team for the benefit of the whole school. Of equal importance for the effective management of teams in secondary schools is the extent to which the staff of the schools see themselves as members of a team, whether it is a subject department, a pastoral team or a cross-curricular working party. Such teamwork has to be seen in the context of the new emphasis given by the ERA to school development and the management of resources in order to achieve those objectives which each school has identified for itself.

ACTIVITIES

1 List all the expectations your team may have of you as team leader. What strategies can you identify for meeting these expectations?
2 List all the management skills required to carry out your main role in school. How many of them are found in the list on pages 37–8 in this chapter?
3 Identify ways in which people in different management positions in your school can provide leadership in professional groups.

Chapter 4

Staff teams and their management

The recent legislation relating to education and the changes which it is bringing about in school management have emphasised the need for management through teamwork. This style of management is neither new nor original. Some of the best-run schools have been organised in this way for many years. Nor has recent legislation changed the nature of teamwork although it may well have had an impact on the roles and responsibilities of team members. It is now more important than ever for teams to be clear about their proper functions and the appropriate ways of carrying them out. With this comes a greater emphasis on the need to communicate effectively between and within teams. This will not happen by accident. Teams need to be deliberately and carefully managed. Tasks within the team need to be shared and responsibilities distributed. This does not involve a 'hard' approach to management founded on directing, controlling, commanding and ordering. In a community of professional colleagues, involvement, co-operation, participation, delegation and effective two-way communication are the essence of management. It is important, however, that teamwork is based on good, professional working relationships which may not be the same as good social relationships. In short, this approach to management will need to be based on effective teamwork throughout the school.

WHAT IS TEAMWORK?

The school staff team will have a number of characteristics. It will have a process for discussing its aims and it will seek to identify and achieve common objectives. Whatever its structure the effectiveness of the group will be increased if there is recognition of the importance of agreed perceptions of the task and of a shared achievement of these common objectives. Thus, shared and agreed plans for the development of the school and for the part to be played in that process by identified individuals is important. Each staff team, whether it is the whole staff group working together or a smaller group of colleagues with a shared function, will have to develop working relationships which are consistent with the overall philosophy of the school. These relationships will need to be negotiated within the group. Once these are established, they will need to be managed. Building and managing staff teams is the prime responsibility of the headteacher and senior staff. It is also an important responsibility of any individual teacher who happens to be leading a group of colleagues at any particular time. This is especially true of those in middle management positions in schools, to whom much of the responsibility for team building and managing is normally delegated. Thus, although professional or subject expertise may be the basis of such leadership, the leadership function can only be carried out to its maximum effect if the staff team is consciously built and effectively managed.

In any discussion of team building and managing, an understanding of the nature of teamwork is crucial but seldom considered. It is generally assumed that everyone knows what teamwork is. Thus, when 'staff team' is mentioned teachers are expected to have a shared perception of what that means. Most staffroom discussions of this matter will reveal just how erroneous that assumption is. For example, the prevalent notion of professional or staff development among almost any group of teachers will focus on developing the skills, knowledge and experience of individuals; but the key to successful teamwork is to be found in the way in which groups of teachers work with each other. Teamwork, therefore, extends beyond 'years' or 'departments'. Teams may be cross-curricular or cross-phase, and long-term or short-term staff groupings. Team or group development, therefore, should be seen as no less important than individual development because teamwork means individuals working together to achieve more than they could alone. The success of the school staff team, then, depends not only on the individual skills of its members but on the way the teachers support and work with each other (see Table 4.1).

Teamwork has been described as playing from the same sheet of music. The implication of this statement is that teamwork can build upon the

---

Table 4.1 Teamwork

What is teamwork?
A group of people working together on the basis of:

- Shared perceptions
- A common purpose
- Agreed procedures
- Commitment
- Co-operation
- Resolving disagreements openly by discussion

This will not happen automatically. Teamwork has to be managed if it is to be effective.

---

strengths of individuals and create confidence within the group which individuals on their own may lack. Thus teamwork, which is demanding and time consuming, can help to reduce stress and pressure through the mutual support which it can provide. Within most schools the individual teacher has hitherto been regarded as the focal point for change and innovation and the locus of expertise. It has been argued here that the team – the collection of co-operating colleagues – will increasingly be the focal point of professional activity within the school. Such activity, if it is well managed, may bring significant benefits to individuals, to groups and to the whole school, as Table 4.2 shows. Thus, the collegial approach to management in schools, while it may be developing through force of circumstance, may bring with it some important benefits to schools. For this to happen the nature of teamwork has to be thoroughly understood. Effective teamwork will not happen automatically by placing groups of individuals in a room together with a task to perform. It requires a set of management strategies. These must be employed by the team leader whether she is the headteacher working with the whole staff or one teacher using her expertise in a particular area of the school's work in conjunction with a group of colleagues with responsibility, say, for the same year group. Colleagues may be members of several teams at any one time. Some teams may be temporary with specific and limited tasks such as planning part of an in-service day or a school concert. Others may be permanent, with responsibility for a subject, pastoral duties or part of the functioning of the school such as industry links or TVEI.

These groups are functional teams. They have a task or series of tasks to complete. They will all consist of a number of individuals with their own skills, experience and responsibilities as well as their own levels of commitment, personal concerns, pressures and influences. They will be guided by a team leader who accepts overall responsibility for the development of the team, its aims, the standards which it sets and the results which it

Table 4.2 The benefits of teamwork in the school

- Agreeing aims
- Clarifying roles
- Sharing expertise and skills
- Maximising use of resources
- Motivating, supporting and encouraging members of the team
- Improving relationships within the staff group
- Encouraging decision-making
- Increasing participation
- Realising individual potential
- Improving communication
- Increasing knowledge and understanding
- Reducing stress and anxiety

achieves. The leadership of any such team may not depend on factors such as position in the school, experience or seniority. Team leaders will tend to be those people with direct and relevant expertise. Therefore, the teacher accepting responsibility for leading the work of a particular team – in a subject department perhaps – may be a relatively junior colleague. In that team may be the headteacher or a deputy head as a team member and not a team leader. The leadership will be provided by the teacher with the expertise. It is therefore crucial that all members of staff in schools understand the processes involved in managing and leading teams.

Teamwork is a group of individuals working together towards some common purpose and, in so doing, achieving more than they could alone. The justification for the existence of a working team in any school would seem, therefore, to be self-evident. Few enjoy working in a situation in which they are isolated, alienated, criticised, over-controlled or where they feel frustrated and dissatisfied with their own performance as a teacher or colleague. Successful teamwork can only take place when the team has the facilities required to gather relevant information, to make sound, informed decisions and to implement those decisions. The absence of any of these factors can mean that the team cannot work effectively or that it will not work at all. Lack of individual commitment can have a similar effect and so can a variety of personal issues which are not brought out into the open within the team context. Individuals may have undisclosed aims which they intend to pursue within the working of the team. The effect of such factors can be considerable. It is the responsibility of the team leader to be able to identify such factors and bring them into the open as part of teamwork.

Colleagues will contribute to the team only that which they feel, as individuals, they wish to contribute. This may include their knowledge and skills, but it may also include their dislikes and jealousies, their uncertainties and perceived or real lack of ability or experience. None of these factors needs to present the team leader with insurmountable difficulties provided she is aware of their existence and has strategies with which to manage them. Lack of skill may be overcome with training. Dislikes need to be aired within the team in a sympathetic and controlled way. Jealousies have to be countered by building self-esteem rather than by diminishing the worth of another individual within the team. An effective team leader will recognise that there are a number of psychological processes operating within any team through which colleagues come to identify with the team. These processes can be seen as a useful counterbalance to those factors which may make effective teamwork difficult.

Interaction between the individual and the team may take place on the basis of one or more psychological contracts which the individual may make, consciously or unconsciously, between herself and the team. The interaction may be based on:

(a) *compliance*, that is, the avoidance of some form of punishment or to gain some form of reward such as acceptance by the team. To the extent that the individual wishes to gain the reward or avoid the punishment, she will comply with what the team is doing;

(b) *identification*, that is, the need to find support for some course of action which the individual may wish to pursue and which she regards as being compatible with the activities of the team. The interaction may be based on rationality: on the recognition that the individual does not have to like the advice for this form of contract to be effective;

(c) *internalisation*, that is, the belief that what the team is doing, or how it seeks to perform its functions, is worthy of support and participation.

This latter is the strongest form of contract and the one which is likely to generate the greatest commitment from the team members to the team itself. Nevertheless, the other forms of contract should not be dismissed or disparaged provided that the team leader can identify them, recognise them for what they are and be aware of the limitations which they imply, for it is with bricks such as these that successful working teams are built.

TEAM DEVELOPMENT

Good teamwork needs to be based on an understanding of the different reasons for and ways of participating in a staff team. Each individual will participate to a slightly different extent and for somewhat different reasons depending on the nature of the psychological contract she has made between herself and the team. The effective leader of a staff team has to be aware of these factors. They constrain the extent to which colleagues are prepared to be involved in the workings of the group, but they are not the only factors affecting involvement. The individual factors mentioned in the previous section are also relevant and so is the way in which teachers perceive the staff team itself. People are usually more willing to commit themselves to expending their time and energy on a staff team if they understand clearly what they are doing and why they are doing it. This means that the team leader has to understand and communicate to colleagues the rationale which underpins the work of the staff team. In other words the existence within the school of a clear and agreed approach to education, as formulated in the school's statement of aims and approached through the development plan, is a crucial element in the effectiveness of the staff team.

It will be clear from the way in which the school is organised that the activities of any staff team are only one part of the total work of the school. Realistically, therefore, there are limits to the problems with which it can cope and the issues which it can address. It serves no useful purpose to have an exaggerated view about what is possible within the framework of the working team. For example, neither the team nor its leader can necessarily be held responsible for having the wrong people appointed to the staff. No amount of teamwork can fit a square peg into a round hole. The team can, however, attempt to develop training programmes for those members who may lack certain skills or information. These need not be as elaborate as a fully blown in-service course, but might simply be the provision of an opportunity for an experienced colleague to work with a less experienced one on a particular aspect of school life.

The team cannot necessarily address directly the problems created by a confused or inappropriate organisational structure in which, for example, a particular group is not functioning effectively or, conversely, is too powerful for the good of the whole school. The team can only try to ensure that it achieves as much as it can in the circumstances. Nor can the team deal with situations which are characterised by a lack of overall planning within the school, low morale in the school or in the wider education system, an inappropriate system of rewards and promotions or other similar problems. These are management problems which are not capable of solution within the staff team. They will be part of the context within which the team has to work and over which its members have little or no control. They do not make effective teamwork impossible but they may make it more difficult. What then, is effective teamwork?

An effective team consists of a group of individuals working together in such a way that much of what they do depends upon and overlaps with the activities of others. This interaction must take place smoothly, efficiently and effectively so that the general provision of education within the school is maintained and improved. This is only achieved by a careful consideration of the five main elements of teamwork: the aims and objectives of the team; its procedures; its processes; the ways in which team members relate to those processes; and the ways in which the activities of the team are reviewed and monitored. All teams are concerned about the image which they have of themselves and which others may have of them; about the standards which are set and the results which are achieved; about the extent to which they can improve and develop both and therefore about the extent to which individual needs, as well as those of the team, are taken into account when activities are planned and responsibilities allocated.

All of these concerns crystallise around the nature of the tasks which the team is expected to undertake. In any staff team the members will, to a greater or lesser extent, be aware of what has to be done. Successful teamwork, however, is best achieved when the aims and objectives are clear and when all members subscribe to them. The distinction between aims and objectives in this context is a crucial one.

Aims, in the context of managing a team in any school, are best regarded as being derived from the overall philosophy of the school and are broadly strategic in nature. An appropriate aim for a pastoral team may be to provide guidance for colleagues on developing their teaching in pastoral and social education (PSE). This also needs to be expressed in terms of objectives.

The objectives are statements about what needs to be done, by whom, with whom, by when, to what standard of proficiency and what should be done as a result. These are the tasks of the team. Each team member should understand exactly what is required of her, and should be informed about the scale and urgency of the task to be carried out. It should not be assumed that team members have this information. The leader of the team should accept the responsibility for providing that information, for checking that it has been assimilated and understood, and for ensuring that the appropriate actions are taken. This is not an intrusion on the professional autonomy of colleagues but, rather, an essential part of the process of effective team management. Nothing inhibits successful teamwork more than the perception, whether accurate or not, that a member of a team is failing in her responsibilities to colleagues or pupils. It is rare indeed for any teacher to believe that she is culpable in this respect. Staff teams will respond to a situation in which the nature of the task to be undertaken is discussed, agreed and fully understood especially when outstanding disagreements about these matters are resolved before any action has to be taken.

Teams of teachers in schools will tend to operate in somewhat different ways according to their circumstances. The different mix of individuals who make up the teams and the nature of the larger organisation, which in this case will be the whole school, all affect the functioning of the team. It is important to recognise that teams cannot exist independently of each other, or of the school itself. Nor should they seek to do so. The team's preferred way of working should be clearly understood by all members. It might be that the team is organised on an open, fully participative basis. Alternatively, it might be firmly and directly controlled by the team leader. The preferred method of operating for many teams is somewhere between those extremes. It will be based on a policy of encouraging all team members to be involved in decision-making where appropriate, but within a clear and specific policy framework based on the school's overall philosophy, aims and objectives as identified in the development plan and negotiated with and agreed by the team members.

The extent to which it is appropriate to involve team members will depend on such factors as the nature of the immediate task. Does it require quick decisions and action? To what extent does it demand clear direction or arouse much emotion? When clear direction is required or when the issue is emotive, too much participation can be counterproductive. Who is affected by the issue or task? Where several team members are affected by the task it is essential to involve all of them in key decisions. Where several team members have knowledge, experience or even an interest in a particular task or issue then it may not be necessary to involve all of them. The appropriate method of operating, therefore, might be on the basis of a predetermined view about who should be involved or about who should take the decision to involve other team members. A team leader who has the trust and respect of the team will be able to carry out this function effectively and ensure that the team can adopt procedures for taking decisions and carrying out tasks. The team can then concentrate on the process of achieving results.

If the procedures adopted by the team dictate how the individuals in that team operate as a group then the processes it uses will influence how it sets about achieving its objectives, getting the results and attaining the standards which it has set itself. The process of task achievement should start by ensuring that all the members of the team fully understand the aims and the objectives. Once established, the objectives need to be divided into tasks, and resources allocated to those tasks. As part of the aim to improve PSE teaching, one objective may be to investigate resources. One task related to this objective will be to look at the use being made of textbooks and work sheets. To achieve this task it is necessary to decide how and by whom the monitoring will be done. Thus the team has moved from an aim, through the stage of identifying relevant objectives, to breaking objectives down into a series of tasks and onto task implementation. Identifying and carrying out those tasks are part of the process of teamwork. The team is already into the realm of planning. Planning is simply a matter of identifying what has to be done, by whom, with what resources and to what time scale. It involves allocating tasks so that everyone within the team knows who is responsible for what.

With those responsibilities should go the necessary authority to ensure that the task can be completed successfully. Resources, both human and material, must be analysed, known and allocated in order to meet the requirements of the various tasks in the most effective way possible. All too often tasks are allocated and resources deployed on the basis of tradition and common practice rather than on the basis of what is actually needed to complete the task in hand. Timing, similarly, is important. Time is always at a premium and it needs managing. One team member's deadline may be another's start time. If the deadline is not met then the next task may not be completed on time. If, for example, the review of existing equipment and the identification of existing textbooks and work sheets are not completed on time then it becomes very difficult for the colleague who has to monitor equipment use to carry out her responsibility. If this is not done, then it will not be possible for recommendations about the future purchase of equipment to be considered. It is worth ensuring, therefore, that the team member responsible for achieving this particular objective knows how this task fits into the overall programme. One member of the team may, as a routine function, ensure that the various schedules are met; a timekeeper, in fact, should be identified. Carrying out the plans, then, requires good communication but it also requires that team members should listen to each other, be supportive and allow ideas and suggestions to be generated and used where possible.

Once the task has been completed this process should still continue. Time should always be allocated so that the team can review what has been done. Team review is a valuable learning and team development activity. All of the team members should be involved in discussing such questions as:

- Did we complete the task successfully?
- What went well in our process and can be repeated next time?
- What went badly and held us back?

It is because these questions are important to present activities as well as for the future development of the team that all team members should be present at such discussions even if their roles were only marginal to the enterprise being considered.

The tasks of any team may change over time, especially if the team is based on year grouping or on a subject that is in a state of change. The processes to be applied in any given situation may vary somewhat from that described but it is important to remember that the tasks of the team form only one dimension of teamwork. The membership of the team is of crucial significance because it transcends any single set of tasks and tends to persist over time. Commitment to, or membership of the team may vary according to the issue or the task. Colleagues will devote more energy to that which they think is important. They will also give their time if they believe that they can influence outcomes or that they have something of value to offer. Membership of the team should be regarded as a variable which may need to be taken into account, reconsidered, developed and cultivated. Team members may need encouraging, reassuring and appreciating in order to establish and retain their membership in an active sense.

The effective team leader has to be aware of these recurring factors and, over a period of time, needs to ensure that the various members of her team feel themselves to be a valuable part of that team. This can be done simply and informally by observing how far team members feel able to relax in the team meetings; how far they have private reservations about team decisions; how far they really accept and understand team objectives; how well the team operates as a group and to what extent influence is shared by all team members or is concentrated in the hands of a very small number of colleagues. The effective team leader will be able to collect much of the information implied in these questions by observation, not by interrogation. In the same way the team leader will recognise the extent to which responsibility is really shared within the team and the degree to which differences within the team are suppressed and denied or are identified and worked through satisfactorily. However, the team can only be strengthened and developed by open discussion of such vital matters.

Team membership can be regarded as the single most significant variable in the development of a successful team. It has to be seen for what it is, a variable rather than a constant. It has to be kept under review if the team is to remain effective. Thus, for any staff team in any school four elements are essential for effective team development. Objectives need to be agreed, shared, clearly understood and subdivided into a number of tasks. Procedures for decision-making and planning should involve all team members. The resulting processes for carrying out tasks should be clear to all team members. These procedures should be reviewed frequently in terms of how far they are facilitating the achievement of team objectives at that time (see Table 4.3).

All individuals bring to the team certain strengths and needs. The combinations may vary but the categories remain the same. Maslow (1954) identified five factors which influence the extent to which colleagues are committed to a team and which help to determine the nature of that commitment. Colleagues might, for example, have basic needs related to survival and existence. Such people will obviously be motivated by the need to earn money and, to the extent that they feel their rewards are just, they can be expected to function reasonably well. When, for example, a significant number of people feel that their rewards are not just, or conditions being imposed are unacceptable, then motivation may depend directly on changes related to basic rewards. Closely related to this is the need for safety and security. This is an especially powerful need when closure, re-organisation or redundancy threaten. Higher order needs can only motivate after these lower order needs have been satisfied. If teachers feel that their jobs are under threat they will not be concerned with esteem, status or professional development.

The third, fourth and fifth categories constitute what Maslow (1954) termed the higher order needs. These are the need for an acceptable self-image. Team members can be helped to become valuable team members by helping them to become the people that they want to be. Few people want to exist in isolation and most value being a member of a group.

Table 4.3 Developing the staff team

Team development

Objectives	The objectives of the team should be clearly understood by all members.
Procedure	All team members should be involved in making important decisions.
Process	All team members should be clear about what has to be done, by whom, by when, with what resources.
Review	The team should review its work regularly as part of a development process.

The fourth category is the need to do something useful or meaningful. Clearly this is related to self-image but it does point out to the team leader that effective team management depends on understanding what colleagues want as much as knowing what the team objectives are. Fifth is the need to grow and develop. This can be a firm basis on which to build team membership. This is particularly true when the team can also provide the opportunity for personal development and, in so doing, meet the need to grow and develop which is experienced by most people. This need is recognised in pupils and is often expressed in terms like fully stretching them or allowing them to reach their full potential. Teachers have a similar need. A good team leader will be aware of that and manage to provide opportunities for team members to grow as part of the team's activities.

McClelland (1961) restated these higher order needs as first, the need for achievement. Colleagues who have this need will like to take personal responsibility, will value succeeding through their own efforts and will welcome feedback on how they are performing. Second, the need for affiliation. This leads colleagues to be concerned with developing and maintaining group relationships rather than with decision-making and task achievement; third, the need for power which finds expression in a desire to achieve results by working through other people. This formulation shows that, apart from financial reward, it is possible to provide rewards in several different ways. Those directly related to achievement might include:

- giving more responsibility, a more interesting activity, freedom to plan and implement, or a change in working conditions such as office space in which to work;
- providing more opportunity to express a particular talent, the chance to develop or improve knowledge or skill, or the chance to exercise full control over some aspects of the team's activities.

Those related to affiliation will include:

- giving approval, co-operation, friendship;
- providing opportunities to work with, to help and to support colleagues within the team.

The need for power can be met by:

- giving opportunity for planning and implementing a long-term or medium-term project;
- involving in broader management of the team and/or the school;
- giving responsibility for part of the work of colleagues.

These possibilities all provide the team leader with opportunities to manage her team to obtain the best effect, both for the individual and the group, while also achieving team objectives.

The importance for effective team management of being clear about the nature of the task has been emphasised throughout this chapter. Setting clear and attainable objectives for the team, allocating responsibilities within it, identifying targets and establishing ways of measuring its progress towards meeting those targets are all part of the duties of the team manager. Planning to ensure that the group attains the success which its members would not otherwise achieve either as individuals or without the management skills of the team leader is, therefore, a crucial part of the role of the effective staff team manager. Central to this is the ability to identify, define and communicate the nature of the tasks to the team members. Equally important are the ability to explain why the team is performing the tasks which have been identified and the flexibility to redefine tasks and encourage the team to reallocate responsibilities and resources when this becomes necessary. A plan is only good as long as it is relevant and is taking the team where the team wishes to go. Management, in this context, includes the ability to recognise when things are going wrong as well as knowing when they are going right.

When things are going right the essential task of the team leader is to maintain the team and ensure that it continues to work together as a co-operative, supportive entity in its own right. With encouragement this will usually happen but, at times, things do go wrong. When this happens it is frequently explained away by the glib phrase 'conflicting personalities', implying that team members are so different and difficult that hostility is endemic and conflict is inevitable. This extreme form of social determinism appears to have very little validity in real situations since it is possible to improve most situations. It might be more useful to view any threat to team co-operation in terms of a conflict of expectations rather than of personalities. Whenever the behaviour of one person violates the expectations of another it can reasonably be anticipated that co-operation may be withdrawn and conflict result. People will then attempt to hurt or punish colleagues rather than help or support them. In such a situation the team leader has to recognise what is happening and maintain the integrity of the team. This will, more often than not, have to be done by helping team members to explore their own behaviour with the intention of highlighting where the conflict in expectation is located but without attempting to attribute blame. Such team maintenance activities are the third dimension of effective team management in the school.

The final dimension of effective team management is the recognition that the leadership role will be different as the nature of the team's activities change (Adair 1983). For example, as already argued, the team will need firm and clear management when it has to complete a specific task within a limited period of time. Alternatively, when the team is exploring ideas and issues the emphasis needs to be on encouraging all colleagues to contribute and drawing contributions together in order to build upon them. At a briefing session, for example, the leader's skills of exposition, checking understanding and the management of information are of prime importance. Persuasiveness, openness and patience combined with the perceptiveness to recognise the importance of what is not being said as well as what is being said are also essential when reviewing.

These four elements – the individuals, the task, the team and the leadership role – have to be balanced by the effective manager of the staff team. This requires an understanding of the individuals in the team, an awareness of what is going on in the group, the skills to act upon this knowledge, and the recognition that different actions might be appropriate in different circumstances. If members are strongly motivated to achieve results, if the team has shared standards and targets, if colleagues seek ways to improve their processes through co-operation and if individuals gain in confidence and ability through belonging to the team and contributing to its success, then the team leader has gone a considerable way towards ensuring that the basic elements of effective team management are all receiving attention.

It is still necessary to build on this, however. The team leader may have a duty to assist colleagues in their own professional development as part of and as an extension to the work of the team. This is related to delegation, but it must also involve some consideration of the career aspirations of team members. Team leaders need to consider these aspirations and try to allocate at least some of the duties within the team to help equip those colleagues to further those aspirations. Team leaders have a responsibility to broaden and expand the experience of staff in order to prepare them for their next promotion. The delegation and organisation of work within the team ought to be structured with this in mind. Team leaders at every level should maximise opportunities to develop colleagues and to assist them in gaining valuable and necessary experience to fit them for promotion whether this is within the school or elsewhere. Such professional staff development can only take place if team leaders set aside time to talk to colleagues about their own development. Some team leaders may wish to initiate regular, although possibly not frequent, and relatively formal discussions with colleagues while others may prefer to leave colleagues to take the initiative. From September 1992 such discussions may be subsumed under a regular cycle of teacher appraisal (DES 1991). However such discussions come about, they need to be given the same detailed attention that would be given to interviewing pupils or parents.

As with all other aspects of managing the team, however, the professional development function has to be seen within the context of the school as a whole. Teams do not work in isolation. They need to communicate with each other and to act as part of the whole school. The team will not control all aspects of its work since much of what it has to do will be circumscribed by school policy. As was seen in chapter 2 this policy is rooted in the school's statement of aims. This, in turn, contributes to the school's development plan which establishes curriculum, staff development, resourcing and management priorities for one, two or three years. The development plan creates the framework within which staff teams in the school are managed and resourced. It is to the formulation of that development plan that we turn in the next chapter.

ACTIVITIES

1 Identify two situations in which your staff team worked well together and completed its tasks or attained its objectives. Why was this so? Identify two situations in which your staff team failed to work well together or successfully to complete its tasks or attain its objectives. Why was this so? What are the main differences in the two sets of circumstances and what forces are working in favour of producing an effective team?

2 List the main tasks of your team. List the main strengths of your team members. Identify which team members can tackle the main tasks. Identify which team members need help with their professional development.

3 This chapter examines the four key elements in effective team management. Under each of the four headings – individual team members, task, team and leadership – list your own strengths and weaknesses; ask a colleague to identify your strengths and weaknesses; identify strategies for building on your strengths; and plan a training programme for yourself to strengthen your weaknesses.

Chapter 5

Developing the school

It was argued in chapter 1 that prior to the mid-1970s secondary schools tended to be managed by the headteacher alone, but with the increase in size and complexity schools began to establish several layers of management. The head was supported by the senior management team. Middle management posts grew as subject departments, faculties, house or year groups emerged. With TVEI and GRIST came co-ordinating roles with cross-curriculuar and, often cross-school responsibilities. Some of these posts carried considerable administrative burdens including the managment of a sizeable budget. In order to co-ordinate the work that went on at these different levels schools needed to have a clearly articulated philosophy, 'the ability to articulate a coherent framework, a set of over-arching goals which meant something to the members of the whole school community' (Jones 1987: 9).

This has become the statement of aims that schools are now required to produce (DES 1989d) and display in their handbook for parents. This was the start of strategic planning in secondary schools. In order to plan strategically senior staff and governors in schools have to take account of:

- the total range of the school's activities;
- the identification of the long-term, and possibly medium-term direction in which they wish the school to move;
- the matching of these intentions, and the school's activities, to the environment and wider community;
- the allocation of finite resources to priorities derived from these long-term intentions for the school;
- the continued monitoring of progress over time.

The key elements in strategic planning for schools, therefore, are analysis, choice, implementation and evaluation. It is from such strategic planning that teams within schools derive their own objectives and identify their own tasks. Increasingly the resources that are allocated to different teams within the school will be determined by such strategic planning. The mechanism for this planning and for the related resource deployment is the development plan that each school will produce.

Headteachers, staff teams and governors, since they have overall responsibility for the curriculum and for the budget in the school, have to find a way of deploying the resources available to that school in order to maximise the learning opportunities for their pupils. They have to establish and own a clear perception of what the school actually stands for. They must share the same vision. As we saw in chapter 2, staff teams and governors must have debated, negotiated and written a statement of aims for their school which encapsulates this sense of mission and shared philosophy. The statement of aims provides the foundation upon which the school's development plan must be built.

The school development plan is a formulated statement setting out the route through which the school will pass in order to achieve its aims. It will usually reflect the findings of a complete or partial review of the school and its resources. It will indicate the short-term, medium-term or long-term achievable targets for all staff and departments. It will contain and plan for the professional development of teachers, so that the existing staffing profile moves closer to the ideal required to deliver the curriculum envisaged in the development plan. If historic LEA policies on the levels of employment of non-teaching staff have been constrained through lack of money, and inappropriate staff in schools have had to perform clerical tasks in the past, the school development plan will indicate the strategies necessary to redress the situation. It will also specify those areas of the school premises which need to be developed in order to maximise their potential. Thus, it is a summary of a school's plans over time, combining curriculum planning with financial planning, planning for staff development, and site and buildings planning.

It has been suggested that there are significant benefits to be gained by schools when they produce a development plan. These include:

- a focus on the aims of education, especially the learning and achievement, broadly defined, of all pupils;
- the provision of a comprehensive and co-ordinated approach to all aspects of planning, one which covers curriculum and assessment, teaching, management and organisation, finance and resources;
- the translation of long-term vision for the school into manageable short-term goals. The priorities contained in the plan represent the school's agenda for action;
- the exercise by teachers of greater control over change rather than feeling controlled by it;
- a greater recognition of the achievements of teachers in promoting innovation and change so that their confidence rises;
- an improvement in the quality of staff development, as in-service training and appraisal help the school to work more effectively and teachers to acquire new knowledge and skills as part of their professional development;

- the strengthening of partnership between the teaching staff and the governing body;
- the simplification of reporting on the work of the school.

(adapted from Hargreaves *et al.* 1989)

A school's development plan will therefore enable the school to concentrate on its defined priorities and to identify ways in which available resources can most effectively be deployed to this end. It will help the school to bring together staff development proposals, curriculum decisions and its responses to national and local priorities. It is an integral part of a continuous process of monitoring and reviewing the school's activities and, as such, can help in the dissemination of good practice throughout the school and beyond. Once formulated, it will provide a vehicle for informing parents of the school's intended direction and informing staff of current priorities and future plans, not least in the area of staff development.

THE CYCLE OF SCHOOL DEVELOPMENT

The implication of this approach to planning is that the development plan will be constructed with the aims of the school as its main point of reference. Figure 5.1 shows that the construction of the plan is, in fact, a cyclical process involving eight stages. All the staff in the school must be aware of the key elements of the school's development plan and be able to recognise how they can make a contribution to it.

A school development plan is a flexible instrument to support the management of the school. It is a cyclical process, not a finished product and operates over a three-year period with targets for the first year being very specific, those for the second year less so, and only broad indications of intent given for year three. There are several essential features of the planning process.

(a) The school needs to have a statement of aims which identifies the essential purpose of the school and guides all those in the school as they carry out their various duties. This will have to be succinct and practical, not based on some vague philosophy or on some unattainable ideal.

(b) The school will have to know what it is already doing and how well it is functioning. It will require, therefore, a regular process of self-review or audit.

(c) As a result of analysing this audit, priorities can be established for the next phase of development planning and, if necessary, the statement of aims can be revised.

(d) The plan, when constructed, will identify a manageable number of development priorities and establish a time-scale for meeting them. It will also show how resources, including finance, time and the professional development of all the staff of the school will be organised to help achieve the priorities in the development plan.

(e) These will be further subdivided into target outcomes or precise objectives together with a clear indication of how and by when they are to be achieved.

(f) The objectives will be expressed in terms of tasks to be performed by particular people within the school, perhaps working with colleagues from outside the school such as consultants, inspectors or advisers.

(g) Criteria for evaluating how far the tasks have been achieved, resources adequately and appropriately deployed and professional development programmes effectively carried out will be built into the plan. These criteria and the evaluation which is based on them will then form the starting point for the next audit. One of the most significant features of this stage will be the evaluation of the teachers' professional development programme, since staff development is crucial if the plan is to be successful.

We can see from Figure 5.1 that the school development plan is not to be constructed in isolation from other external factors. Initiatives from elsewhere in the education system will impinge on the planning as will the availability of resources, the demands of parents and the priorities of members of the school's wider community.

This cycle of school development planning makes the assumption that schools grow most effectively from within rather than as a result of external directives. To the extent that staff feel that they own and control their school's developments they will be committed to them. Furthermore, the very act of development planning can build and support teams within the school and provide valuable professional development opportunities. When resources are perceived to be inadequate, however, this will not be the case. Development planning can, nevertheless, help schools to make more soundly based judgements about their levels of resourcing and how best to allocate what is available.

School development is a process of reviewing, reconsidering, setting priorities, allocating resources, defining and completing tasks and evaluating outcomes. There are four basic activities that combine to make up the total development planning process. These are:

- carrying out an audit or review to establish the school's strengths and to identify opportunities for change and development from which priorities will be selected;
- formulating a plan which establishes priorities, targets and tasks over an agreed time-scale;
- implementing the plan within the limits of available resources;
- evaluating the success of the implementation and reviewing the priorities for the next time period.

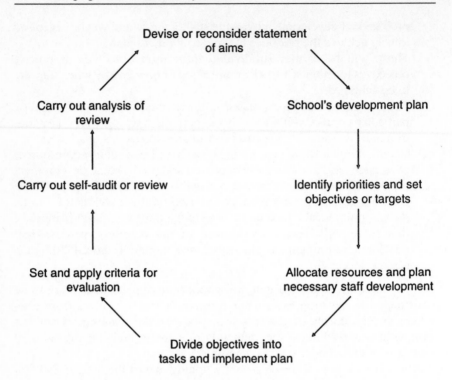

Figure 5.1 The school development cycle

This process may start with the school's statement of aims. Some schools may construct this statement using a process similar to that outlined in chapter 2. If the school has a statement then it may, at times, need to reconsider it, especially if the circumstances within the school or in its wider community change significantly. Whether the statement is established or is being revised, it is essential that all staff, working in teams, have an opportunity to become involved and that the governors are treated as important partners in the process since it is they who are responsible for the long-term policies that the school must adopt.

THE AUDIT

If, as suggested, the statement of aims is firmly rooted in what the school already does, a review or audit will be required to establish what exactly are the strengths of the school and to identify areas for future development. One approach to this was outlined in chapter 2, but staff teams and governors may wish to adopt a somewhat different approach based on five simple questions. These are:

- Where is the school now?
- What changes need to be made in the school?
- How best can these changes be managed over time?
- What are the resource implications of these proposed changes?
- How can it be shown that the changes have been managed successfully?

Hargreaves *et al.* (1989) suggest that it is impossible for a school to carry out a full and detailed audit every year. Therefore, they argue, a school might select any of the following areas for intensive audit in a single year:

- pupils' diversity and achievements;
- assessment and recording;
- teaching styles and methods;
- responsibilities of the teaching staff;
- school management and organisation;
- relationships with parents;
- partnership with the local community;
- links with other schools and colleges;
- school, LEA and national documents.

(adapted from Hargreaves *et al.* 1989: 6–7)

They also suggest that two further areas require an annual audit because of their importance. These are the curriculum and the school's resources. As schools face the task of implementing the National Curriculum, dealing with the new programmes of study, seeking to achieve attainment targets and to link those to GCSEs, the curriculum audit is obviously a necessity. Therefore schools need to:

- check whether the planned curriculum meets the statutory requirements;
- identify possible gaps or overlap between subject areas;
- ensure that where two or more subjects or activities are concerned with the same range of objectives, this is recognised and used positively and that joint planning takes place [where possible];
- analyse the curriculum for each year group in terms of curricular objectives within and outside the National Curriculum bearing in mind especially the attainment targets at the relevant key stages;
- decide in which parts of the school curriculum to locate work leading to the National Curriculum and other school curricular objectives;
- assess how much teaching time is available and how best to use it, considering alternatives to present provision;
- compare planned provision with actual provision;
- judge whether curriculum issues need to be among the priorities for development.

(adapted from Hargreaves *et al.* 1989)

As for the auditing of resources, this too, is an obvious necessity especially as schools establish ways to manage delegated budgets. There needs to be an appropriate match between plans for development and the utilisation of resources. Account, therefore, needs to be taken of:

- how and why the school used its resources during the previous year;
- how the school judges and ensures effective and efficient use of resources;
- how development planning should fashion the use of resources rather than being fashioned by them at a late stage;
- the use made of the expertise and time of teachers and support staff;
- expenditure on materials, consumables and equipment;
- running costs such as heating, lighting, telephone bills;
- the use of resources from outside the school's immediate budget e.g., TVEI, GEST;
- resources or income the school has generated (and may be able to generate) for itself;
- the use of accommodation.

(Hargreaves *et al*. 1989: 7)

At the same time larger schools, or those with a high staff turnover in certain areas, may wish to carry out a more detailed staffing audit. Table 5.1 suggests a series of questions that might be asked. This might be done at department, faculty or whole-school level. It will be noted that both teaching and administrative staff are included in the audit. Where appropriate, technical and other support staff should also be included.

If such a complex audit is to be carried out in a relatively short space of time it will have to be carefully planned. Questions arise such as how to identify appropriate areas for audit and how to collect, compile and present information and to whom to present it. This type of activity is best done in small teams in which the team leader has a clear and limited brief with a specific time scale and defined resource limits within which to work. The team should produce a short summary statement of the main findings and recommended areas for development with a concise statement of the reasons for the proposals. The headteacher or senior member of staff can then bring the different elements of the audit together by producing an overview which lists the main issues, the main areas for possible development and the reasons for them. This can then be discussed in the appropriate groups such as staff teams and the senior management team. Ultimately the headteacher will need to formulate a proposal which identifies a limited number of priorities for year one of the plan with others provisionally suggested for years two and three. These proposals will then have to be discussed and agreed by the governors before the development plan itself can be finalised.

CONSULTING THE PLAN

The results of the audit or review provide valuable information on which the school's development plan can be based, but this information should not be considered in isolation. The plan will be influenced by a wide range of other factors, some of which may emerge as part of the audit but some of which

---

Table 5.1 A staffing audit

Teaching staff

What skills are required to implement the school's development plan?
What are the staffing implications?
Compare these with the existing staffing profile.
What are the implications:
For forward planning?
e.g. – known retirements
  – increase [or decrease] in budget share
For unplanned forward planning?
e.g. – staff promotions or departures
     For the curriculum?
     For timetabling?
     For use of allowances?
     For the allocation of resources?
     For INSET and staff development?

Administrative, technical and other support staff

List the resources available.
Draw a sketch plan of the working areas indicating key work stations,
  machinery, IT, filing areas, desks, photocopier, telephones.
List the main tasks undertaken by administrative, technical and support staff.
List the non-child contact tasks undertaken by teaching staff.
List the informal tasks regularly undertaken.
Match tasks, done and anticipated, with job descriptions.

Evaluation

Is correct use being made of existing staff?
Is best use being made of the space available?
Are more non-teaching staff required?
Are other resources required?
Given the flexibility of LMS, do staff or resources need to be re-allocated?
Should different or additional staff be employed in order to meet school
  objectives more effectively?
What are the implications for the school development plan?

---

may not. In Figure 5.2 many of these factors are shown. When the plan is constructed, account needs to be taken of the national and LEA initiatives as well as of the school's own concerns. At the same time there will be community issues relevant to the school that may be articulated by governors or other stakeholders in the school. Similarly there may have to be educational, organisational or managerial changes in the school in order to cope with new initiatives or to confront new problems. All of these factors have to be taken into account when formulating the development plan. One LEA has proposed to its schools a staged process for arriving at a school development plan. The stages are:

1 Examine the purposes and positive advantages for the school of the development plan.
2 Assess the school's strengths and weaknesses with all stakeholders concerned; staff, governors, parents, pupils, local and feeder schools and nurseries, future employers and the community.
3 Pool information and decide on priorities for the school.
4 Assess and cost resources and materials needed.
5 Construct detailed plan and allocate roles, responsibilities and other involvement.
6 Identify INSET needs and plan staff development.
7 Focus on the financial allocation for the school under formula funding. Can the plan be carried out with existing resources? Does extra income need to be generated?
8 Identify and cost outside support needed.
9 Decide time plan, including regular review.
10 Prepare contingency plan for the unexpected.
11 Implement the plan.
12 Review before next cycle.

(adapted from City of Birmingham Education Department 1990)

The essence of the development plan is the identification of priorities and the translation of these into objectives or targets and then into a series of tasks to be carried out. If this is done, as it should be, for a period of no less than three years then the priorities and targets for the first year should be very precisely defined and the tasks and related resources specifically identified and allocated. For any one year there should be only an achievable number of priorities, say a maximum of three. For the second year this process can be less defined but must nevertheless be clearly and carefully done. The identification of priorities for the third year may be more speculative and the tasks expressed in more general terms. As time goes by and the plan is implemented, then the priorities and tasks for the later years become more precisely defined and new ones added for subsequent years. Thus a rolling programme of development can be established.

Constructing the plan is based on the identification of developmental priorities for a period of years but these must be agreed within the school and by governors. The plan needs to contain clear statements about who is responsible for what task and what action will be taken. The formulation of objectives and the identification and achievement of tasks will be dealt with in more detail in the next chapter. The tasks and targets of the school's development plan, however, do not exist in isolation. Steps have to be taken to link this plan to other aspects of school planning such as resource planning, staff development and management development. Finally the plan must be publicised since it is a public document as well as a working document. In its public form the plan should include:

- the school's statement of aims;
- the proposed priorities and time-scale for achieving them;
- a brief justification for the priorities in the context of where the school is now and where it wants to get to;
- an indication of how the development plan links in with other planning such as staff development;
- an action plan for each priority;
- an indication of the resource implications of the plan;
- a statement about how the plan will be evaluated and by whom;
- a description of the methods to be used to report outcomes.

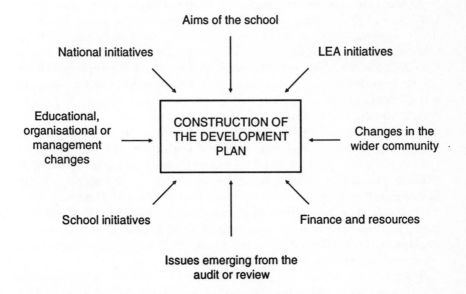

Figure 5.2 Factors influencing a school's development plan

Source: adapted from Hargreaves *et al.* 1989: 10.

Implementing the plan

Implementing the school development plan requires the use of all the skills of team management that were discussed in the previous chapter, especially the ability to motivate staff and to generate and sustain commitment to the plan as it affects individual members of the team. Since no one person can implement an entire plan, delegation is also an important aspect of implementation. This, together with the setting of clear and precise targets, will be discussed in the next chapter. However skilful a team leader is, constructing a plan is far easier than implementing it. When the plan contains a clear statement about priorities, targets that are identifiable and achievable, a strategy for allocating and utilising available resources, and specific success criteria, then the process of implementation becomes a little easier.

If the development plan is well constructed it will state clearly a limited set of priorities, each of which will have a related number of objectives or targets. These show the way to successful implementation since they enable team leaders to see how progress is being made towards particular objectives. Many of the actions that need to be taken as part of the day-to-day process of implementation are precisely those which an effective team leader will normally be doing: encouraging and supporting staff, facilitating their professional development and evaluating progress. This will all be done in the context of agreed targets, a set of tasks that are delegated to members of the team and a known budget.

As will be seen in the next chapter, well written targets will contain a clear indication of the relevant success criteria. Evaluating the extent to which these success criteria are being met is a crucial part of implementation. In other words the processes of implementation and evaluation are closely linked. Evaluation does not take place at the end of the implementation period, but is an integral part of the implementation process. In fact, as far as school development plans are concerned, progress-checking is a more accurate description of what happens than the usual term, evaluation.

Hargreaves *et al.* (1989) use the term 'interlaced' to describe the relationship between implementation and evaluation. They suggest that, because different priorities and their related targets will require action over different time scales, there is no single time in the school year when the implementation process could or should be evaluated. Therefore, they argue, evaluation should be a continuous process that helps to shape and guide implementation because, however good a plan is, it will not be implemented automatically. Thus, successful implementation requires both continued support and regular progress-checking.

Team leaders will need to show that they are interested in the progress that is being made within the team and by individuals. For all team leaders and especially senior staff it is important that this interest finds visible expression through:

- ensuring that, as far as is possible, tasks are properly delegated, distributed fairly and enable colleagues to satisfy their own motivational needs in the ways outlined in the previous chapter;
- making regular but occasional informal enquiries about progress;
- providing opportunities for colleagues to talk over what they are doing in an informal setting, thus giving the opportunity for reporting actual or anticipated problems;
- being available at regular intervals to talk through progress in a more formal setting;
- attending meetings occasionally, particularly if they may be able to provide advice, support or outside help.

  This is important for senior staff, who may have a broader view or more access to resources than members of a particular team. It is also part of the role of the team leader of, say, a department in which several working parties are operating.

Team leaders continually need to ask questions such as:

- How well are we doing so far?
- What have we achieved so far?
- Which of our objectives have we met so far?
- Have we met any of our objectives?
- Are we keeping to deadlines?
- Is any revision of our plan needed?
- Do we need to be more effective?
- Are we managing within the allocated resources?
- Is there anything that we no longer need to do?

These are all progress-checking questions. Checking on progress is the direct responsibility of the team leader but it can be delegated to somebody else in the team. Progress should also be reviewed regularly as a normal part of team meetings and has three advantages. First, if progress-checking is a normal part of the procedure it becomes far less threatening for any individual or group to be told that progress is not being made. Progress-checking should be seen as part of the continuous pattern of delegating responsibilities. Second, regular progress-checking can help to identify potential problems before they happen or catch small problems before they become large ones. Third, if sufficient progress has been made it is easier to make sensible decisions about the next step. It may even be possible to reduce the work load or to find quicker ways of operating.

It would be unrealistic to assume that implementation always goes according to plan and that objectives are always achieved. Circumstances may change during implementation. Estimates about the time or resources needed might have been inaccurate, unexpected obstacles may be encountered, staff changes or illness may have occurred. Policy changes beyond the control of the school may also influence the availability of resources. For these and many other reasons it might be necessary to make changes in the plan. Such changes might include:

- providing extra support or extra resources for the team or for individuals within the team;
- changing the time-scale;
- reorganising to concentrate on fewer priorities or on a more limited number of targets for a particular priority;
- postponing a priority or substituting a different one;
- agreeing to take no further action at this stage in one area with the intention of coming back to it at a later date;
- changing roles and responsibilities within the team or making more use of existing or new expertise within the team;
- providing additional staff development for one or more team members;
- seeking help from elsewhere in the school or from outside the school.

Towards the end of the time allocated for a particular priority the team will need to establish how successful it has been in implementing that part of the plan. Identifying and acknowledging where success has been achieved is a powerful motivator for future plans. Exploring ways of being even more effective will help the team to achieve success in other priority areas. The task of carrying out such a check should be given to a specific person who has responsibility for collecting the available information about the progress that has been made, especially on changes in practice and procedures that have resulted from the plan. Time will need to be allowed for members of the team to discuss this information. A short report on how far each of the targets relating to that priority has been achieved should be written and these should then be combined into a final report for discussion at a team meeting. This will need to focus on the implications for future work.

A similar procedure will need to be followed at school level when the success of implementation of the whole plan is considered. Here, as Hargreaves *et al.* (1989) remind us, the focus will be on how far the pupils' learning and achievement have been affected and the extent to which the school's aims have been furthered. Reports may be made to parents, through the annual parents' meeting or through newsletters or open days, and to governors through the headteacher's report to the governing body and governors' working parties and through their visits to the school. Schools will need to consider how far pupils should be involved in development planning and what mechanisms might be used. At the very least, pupils should be informed about aspects of the plan since they play a role in its implementation. The whole cycle will begin again at this point as staff consider how to disseminate new practices throughout the school and examine the impact of the completed plan on the original priorities for the next two years. At the same time, changes in national and local policies and resource provision will need to be taken into account as well as the changing circumstances of the school.

The development plan is the school's main vehicle for strategic planning. It is derived from the aims of the school and is created to take account of the present circumstances of the school and of those resourcing and policy changes, both internal and external, that can be predicted. The purpose of the plan is to identify priorities for development, to establish targets within those priorities, to define tasks related to those targets and to allocate the responsibility, together with the necessary resources, for accomplishing those tasks. It will be based on a detailed review of the school and its resources and will involve consultation with members of the whole school community.

School development planning is a cyclical process in the sense that it is based on an audit of where the school is now and on the identification of what it wishes to achieve in the next three years. Development planning is cyclical in another sense since it encompasses an ongoing plan over a three-year time-scale. At the end of each planning cycle there is a reporting process that enables the staff of the school as well as the parents, governors and pupils to take stock of what has been achieved and what still needs to be done. This provides the basis for the next school development planning cycle.

This approach to planning is based on the assumption that schools are capable of organic growth from within and that this is best achieved where schools can set their own priorities and manage their own resources. Planning and implementing become corporate activities rather than depending on individuals. Schools are thus not subject to the pitfalls of planning based on what Georgiades and Phillimore have termed:

> the myth of the hero-innovator: the idea that you can produce, by training, a knight in shining armour who, loins girded with new technology and beliefs, will assault his organisational fortress and institute changes both in himself and others at a stroke. Such a view is ingenuous. The fact of the matter is that organisations such as schools will, like dragons, eat hero-innovators for breakfast.
>
> (Georgiades and Phillimore 1975: 134)

Rather, school development becomes a continuous, controlled and systematic process based on priorities, objectives and tasks. The team, rather than the individual, is the important centre of activity. Crucial to this is the ability to determine priorities and to set objectives.

ACTIVITIES

1 If your school already has a development plan:
- examine how far it reflects the school's statement of aims;
- consider to what extent the plan is based on consultation and with whom;
- think through the implications for the plan of carrying out a staff audit such as that in Table 5.1;
- identify the implications of the plan for your team;
- look at ways of using the twelve-stage process for producing the plan that is outlined on page 66;
- identify the main success criteria for your plan as they affect your team and its work;
- list the strategies you intend to use, or are using, to implement the plan;
- list the ways in which you will evaluate the plan;
- identify the appropriate reporting procedures and decide how you will produce your report;
- identify the implications of implementing and evaluating the plan for the next stage or cycle in your development planning.

2 If your school does not already have a development plan:
- if practical, carry out a review or audit of your school or your team to identify your priorities for change;
- carry out a staff audit such as that in Table 5.1;
- formulate your priorities into a development plan using the stages outlined on page 66;
- examine how far the plan reflects the school's statement of aims;
- consider to what extent the plan is based on consultation and with whom;
- identify the implications of the plan for your team;
- identify the main success criteria for your plan as they affect your team and its work;
- list the strategies you intend to use to implement the plan;
- list the ways in which you will evaluate the plan, identify the appropriate reporting procedures and decide how you will produce your report.

Chapter 6

The staff team: Its priorities and their management

School development planning is based on using the school's statement of aims to identify priority areas in which changes will take place over a known and limited time-scale. At best a plan will concentrate on no more than three such priority areas over any one school year. In each of these areas there will be a number of objectives or targets to meet. Again there should only be a limited number of these, say three or four, for any one individual or team. These targets are then further subdivided into tasks which are allocated to individuals or groups. Resources to carry out these tasks have to be identified and allocated, and the whole process monitored and evaluated using a set of agreed success criteria and a specific pattern of reporting. In this process, the staff team derives its own priorities from the school's development plan, identifies the relevant targets and tasks, allocates the resources that it has at its disposal, carries out its monitoring and evaluation and reports its progress. Here the priorities of each team will reflect the priorities of the school.

For this to happen those priorities have to be clearly stated and understood. It is the role of the senior management team to ensure that team leaders understand the nature of the school's priorities and that they are clear about what contribution each particular team has to make to the implementation of the development plan. The team leader, in her turn, must ensure that she understands what part her team has to play in carrying out the plan and what her team's priorities and targets therefore need to be. Resources then have to be managed in order to enable the team to play its part. Not all of a team's priorities will necessarily be derived from the school's development plan. Any staff team, whether this term is used for the whole staff or for a sub-group within the whole staff, is both a functional and a developmental grouping.

It is functional in the sense that the people in the team will be united by sets of common purposes and processes. The team members will have as their major concern the education of the children in their care or, at least, a specific aspect of that education. This concern will result, for the effective team, in the determination of clear and attainable priorities, the appropriate allocation of responsibilities and the measurement of progress towards achievements which are derived from those priorities. The staff team is developmental because it provides a framework within which the professional growth of each of its members may take place. Such professional development may enable a colleague to contribute more to the work of the team or it may provide the foundation for a change of professional direction.

The functional and developmental balance within each staff team will be determined by the circumstances of the individuals within the team and by the situation in which the school finds itself at any particular time. Each school, and each team within each school, will have its own starting point. Thus, the priorities which are established will find expression through the activities of individuals and groups within the school as they address themselves to their professional functions. The priorities which are established are more likely to be met effectively through staff groups acting in concert for all the reasons which have been rehearsed in the previous chapters of this book.

The team leader has to ensure that the priorities of the team and the related targets are clarified and reinforced by identifying the active, positive tasks which the team has to undertake. In order to do this, those in secondary school middle management, as well as those in more senior positions, have to adopt a realistic approach to the allocation of available resources, including staff time. The fair and effective delegation of duties, the establishing and maintenance of communication between team members, and ensuring that all team members are able to make the most effective use of the time available to them are crucial components of resource management.

It has been argued in a previous chapter that management can be thought of as a combination of three distinct but related activities:

- getting things done, or administration;
- doing new things, or innovation;
- reacting to crisis, or salvation.

The management of any school or of any part of any school involves all three forms of activity, but effective management only comes about through establishing the right balance between those activities. Any manager who is perpetually reacting to one crisis after another will hardly be in control of events, let alone be capable of managing an effective team of colleagues. It is not unusual, however, for those in middle and senior management positions in schools to argue that they have time only for crisis management and not for innovation, and the planning and thinking which it involves. The person who has allowed the routine administration to become such a burden that it occupies every available moment is equally at fault, as is the permanent innovator who is always dealing with change and can never establish stability. They are all unable to manage their time.

The ability to do this is essential before anyone can seek to share the responsibility for the work of others. The leader of a team must therefore be capable of managing the time available for the work of that team. Before this can be achieved, however, she needs to be able to organise her own time effectively. In order to do this she will find it helpful to be able to plan her work in terms of objectives or targets to be achieved. Such an approach becomes essential with the advent of development planning and the related requirement to manage resources effectively.

TARGETS AND TASKS

In earlier chapters it has been established that identifying targets based on priorities is part of a process of strategic planning within the school. Any school will take its stance on such planning from its statement of aims, a broad statement of what the school wishes to achieve based on where it is now and what it already achieves. In this context we have seen how priorities are derived from the statement, objectives or targets are established for the priorities, and tasks defined for each target. This is not to say that the whole of school teaching and its planning can be expressed in terms of specific targets to be achieved over an identified period of time. Target setting is a technique which can help in planning and in teaching. Perhaps it can be employed more usefully and effectively than has hitherto been the case for, as Adair (1983) reminds us, a target is visible, tangible and concrete and, therefore, it can become a focus for activity.

Clearly defined targets can help the teacher to know where she is going, to check that she is succeeding in getting there, to organise the necessary resources and to sequence her work appropriately. The same is true of the teams to which she may belong within her school. The essence of a helpful and useful target is that it will contain within its formulation a clear statement about the acceptable criteria for success. Teachers use targets to help them plan their work.

Teachers in an English department that has a particular concern about the reading attainments of its first year intake might set itself the following targets for specific groups of children:

- at the end of the school year all the children in the group will have a reading age which is at least the equivalent of their chronological age;
- at the end of the school year at least half of the children in the group will have a reading age which is one year or more higher than their chronological age;
- at the end of the school year at least one third of the group will have a reading age which is two years or more higher than their chronological age.

These targets should form part of the written plans or forecasts for a department or for individual teachers. Note that they have a number of things in common.

(a) They are clear and specific.
(b) They are quantitative rather than qualitative in that the extent to which success has been achieved can be measured accurately.
(c) They focus on identifiable results rather than on activity.
(d) They are, or should be, realistic to the extent that they are achievable and yet they provide a challenge.
(e) They have a time-scale.
(f) The emphasis is on end results rather than on processes or activities.

They are progresive. It is possible to identify which targets were hit and which were missed. Teams can examine why some were not hit. They may discover, for example, that too much emphasis was placed on achieving the third target or that the first one was unrealistic.

Targets are meaningless unless their achievement or non-achievement can be evaluated. Although targets should be measurable and attainable they should not be so rigid as to restrict or inhibit the work of the school or of individual teachers. Thus, in attempting to achieve the reading targets the teacher may give detailed consideration to the various teaching strategies which she is adopting with particular children in order to improve their reading performance. Should her efforts prove unsuccessful, however, she should not normally be blamed or made to feel that she has failed professionally. Targets are guidelines and not absolute criteria of success in themselves. The reasons for missing targets may well need to be explored but this must be done in a professional, co-operative and supportive manner. If the particular target is of sufficient importance then those involved will want to achieve it and will want to know why it has not been achieved if such is the case. Targets of no real consequence should not be set in the first place.

Targets have been discussed here in the context of teaching and learning, but it is important to recognise that there are several different types of targets with which teachers may be concerned. Trethowan (1987) identifies five types of target:

• targets concerned with teaching and learning and the fulfilling of related responsibilities and with maintaining certain standards;
• targets concerned with the individual teacher's professional or personal development where this has a bearing on school work;
• targets which have to be attained by a group, team or department within the school;
• targets related to major but temporary projects which might be innovations or connected with solving specific problems;
• targets to be achieved by the school staff as a whole either acting in concert or as individuals.

A complete list of such targets should relate to the priorities of the school for that particular period of time.

As we have seen, such long-term planning can take the form of a school development plan. It can also take the form of encouraging school staff to identify three or four targets which they would like to attain in the course of a forthcoming school year. This might be done by individual consultations between a teacher and her team leader or headteacher in the summer term, followed by a team or staff discussion early in the autumn term. Whatever the method used, it is important to ensure that no member of staff is attempting to achieve too many targets. It is also important to see that the short-term targets relate to the targets that have been set for that team over the relevant period of time and that the targets themselves are stepping stones towards fulfilling the priorities of the school. Trethowan (1987) warns that no teacher should be expected to work towards more than six targets at any one time. Given the pressures on teachers as individuals, on groups of teachers within schools and on the schools themselves, three such targets may be a more sustainable number. Much depends on the range of activities being undertaken, but to set between three and six targets is realistic. To demand more than this is to be counter-productive. Expecting too much will achieve nothing. Far better to be clear about the ordering of priorities and thus specific about the identification of targets. It is impossible to achieve everything immediately. A realistic approach to target setting can be a useful technique towards achieving much in a relatively short space of time (see Table 6.1).

For this to happen, however, each target has to be divided into a number

---

Table 6.1 Establishing effective targets

Result:	Does the target define a required result?
	Always define results, not actions to achieve results.
Time-scale:	Does the target include a time-scale?
	If timing is important, it should be included in the target.
Measurable:	Can performance against target be measured or assessed accurately?
	Build in hard measures whenever possible and avoid general or woolly definitions or yardsticks.
Precise:	If the target is precise everyone using it will interpret it in the same way.
Realistic:	Is the target realistic and challenging?
	Do not set ideal performance levels that cannot be achieved.
	Do not set slack performance levels that can be achieved very easily.
Complete:	Does the full set of targets provide a complete picture?
	Make sure that you have included all the key targets to measure total success.

of tasks. The nature of the tasks will depend on the targets. For example, if the objective is to improve pupil performance in GCSE History then the targets might include:

- The GCSE History group will have a 90 per cent pass rate two years from now.
- A minimum of 65 per cent of the group taking GCSE History will obtain a pass at C or above two years from now.

From 1994 the grading for GCSE may change as a result of the introduction of assessment at key stage 4, but the principle of target setting in this way still holds. For some schools these may be relatively low targets but for others they may be very difficult to achieve. For this school they are realistic and attainable yet challenging. Already it can be seen that the targets are specific, measurable, and contain a time-scale and built-in success criteria.

These targets now have to be translated into tasks. Since, in many schools, GCSE History depends heavily on coursework, especially projects, improving the quality of pupils' project writing might be identified as one of the main tasks. This could then be divided into three sub-tasks.

(a) *Improving pupils' study skills.* One team member might be asked to produce and teach a four-hour study skills package for all pupils starting GCSE History. The package would be a combination of lessons and self-study material. It would be ready by the start of the autumn term, would cost no more than £75 to produce and would be aimed specifically at skills relevant to GCSE History.

(b) *Improving pupils' presentational skills.* Another team member could produce a three-hour set of taught material supported by examples of good presentation related specifically to GCSE History projects by the start of the autumn term within a budget of £50.

(c) *Improving the quality of materials that are available to pupils in the History department.* A third team member may examine the existing materials and find ways of improving it within a budget of £200 in the first year and £75 in the two subsequent years.

Each of these sub-tasks can be further subdivided into specific activities. For example, if we take the third task it might be subdivided thus:

- inspect books for relevance to current GCSE curriculum and appropriateness for pupil use (by 20 May);
- remove inappropriate books (after end of summer term);
- inspect other source material for relevance to current GCSE curriculum and appropriateness for pupil use (by 20 May);
- remove inappropriate material (after end of summer term);
- Identify and order new books and other materials that are appropriate, relevant, useful and able to be used by pupils, checking on delivery times (by 1 June or sooner depending on delivery dates);

- check quality of environment with reference to access to and display of material (during June);
- improve environment and display within existing resources (by autumn term);
- identify other potential sources of material such as local visits supported by study guides, material from museums, commercial firms and public companies (by autumn term);
- catalogue available resources and relate to relevant parts of the curriculum (by autumn term).

A reporting procedure might involve informing the team leader of the proposed time-scale for the sub-tasks and telling her of progress at the times when the various tasks should have been completed. This would provide an opportunity to reschedule work, ask for help, obtain support and even to receive praise.

Success criteria for these sub-tasks would include judgement by head of department and colleagues on appropriate use of material; increased pupil use of material; improved quality of use of material in GCSE History projects; an improvement in marks gained by pupils for GCSE History projects; and increased expressions of satisfaction with work by teachers and pupils. In short, success criteria should be derived from a clear understanding by teachers of why they have set specific targets and tasks for themselves and others and of what, precisely, they want to achieve. Such criteria can and should contain both impressionistic, qualitative or subjective elements, such as expressions of satisfaction, and more objective, measurable or quantitative components, such as increased use of materials and improved grades.

In-service support might also be required in the form of a training session to raise the awareness of colleagues about the availability of new books and materials and improved access to them. This might be part of a History staff training day about the whole area of improving the quality of pupils' project writing.

In all this it is necessary to bear five basic questions in mind:

- What do I want or need to accomplish?
- What do I have to do in order to accomplish what I want?
- By when must I have accomplished it?
- How will I know when I have succeeded?
- To whom do I report, how and when?

This may all appear to be very time consuming, but a schematic approach such as that outlined in Figure 6.1 can help. Remember, however, that priorities, targets and tasks are a guide to what needs to be done, by whom, by when and with what resources. No odium should be attached for a failure to complete a task or achieve a target. A more positive approach is to explore

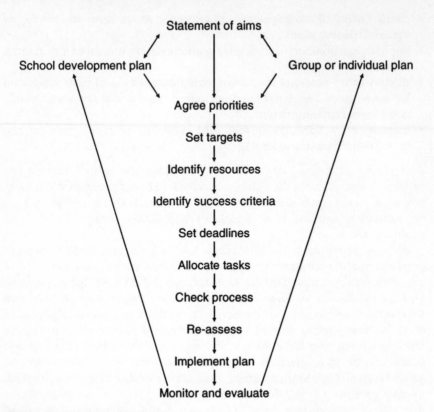

Figure 6.1 Managing priorities

the reasons why the target was not reached or the task not completed and provide the necessary support in the future. Nevertheless, working in this disciplined way is very demanding. It involves sharing responsibility within the team. This means that the team leader has to ensure that those responsibilities are shared equitably between people able to carry out the necessary tasks. This means more than simply allocating responsibilities to people: it means delegating.

DELEGATION

Delegation within the secondary school is inevitable since no team leader or headteacher can possibly do all the necessary work. There are, however, some things which cannot be delegated. As Everard and Morris (1985) point out, common policies, common systems, agreed priorities and targets, and a clear view of what each individual is expected to achieve provide a framework within which effective delegation of tasks can take place. All staff need to be involved in taking decisions about such matters, but at the school level the headteacher has the ultimate responsibility for them. This responsibility cannot be delegated. At the team level, setting the priorities and targets for the team has, ultimately, to be the responsibility of the team leader and so does the organisation of team members.

Delegation is, in a very real sense, a part of staff development. More often than not in schools it is treated as dumping or abdicating – giving away work which a superior does not want to do, cannot do, and cannot bother to train somebody else to do properly. If school tasks were delegated effectively and more frequently then people who gain promotion would already be able to carry out most of the essential duties attached to their new post. It is part of the duty of the team leader to ensure that tasks are delegated effectively especially as delegation involves far more than merely giving another colleague a job to do. It has more to do with the assignment of responsibility and authority than with the transfer of a task from one person to another.

In order to identify which tasks might usefully be delegated, headteachers and team leaders should ask themselves the following questions:

- Which of my tasks can already be done by some or all members of staff?
- Which of my tasks make only a small contribution to the total success of the school?
- Which of my tasks take up more time than I can afford?
- Which of my tasks are not strictly related to my key targets?
- Which of my tasks are really the day-to-day responsibilities of a colleague?
- Which of my tasks cause problems when I am away because nobody else can take them on effectively?
- Which of my tasks would help members of staff to develop if they were given the responsibility?

It is then possible to take this one stage further by listing answers to these questions on the left-hand side of a sheet of paper and then, for each task, asking which of the staff team is likely to be able to carry out that task already, or could be trained for it; which of the staff team might benefit from the experience; who is overloaded and who has a fairly light load. The answers to questions such as these can help to identify those to whom to delegate as well as what to delegate. Be sure that you delegate complete tasks, not just parts of them. These are the first stages in effective delegation (see Table 6.2).

Delegation should never be undertaken without some form of training. Training, in this context, does not necessarily mean that a teacher has to be sent on a long-term secondment or an in-service course. Training needs prior to delegation can and should be met from within the resources of the school. More often than not this should be the role of the team leader or some other experienced colleague. Schools now have much more flexibility in this area since they have available to them limited funds and up to five training days for in-service training each year. These resources are meant to meet much wider demands than those being discussed here. This they may or may not do. Within the context of delegating effectively, however, they do provide schools with some resources to enable colleagues to be prepared adequately for new and different roles. It should be remembered that training need not cost money. Explanation, coaching, demonstration, trial and error in a supervised situation and, 'sitting by Nellie' are all forms of training which have been successfully applied in schools at very low cost. The point is that training should come before delegation and not the other way round.

Successful delegation depends on first, defining clearly and precisely areas of responsibility to be delegated. The purpose of the job to be delegated and the nature of the responsibility should be understood and agreed. Modification to the job description may be required. Hence the importance of discussion and agreement. In any case a number of points need to be made clear. Is the responsibility permanent or does it last for a specific and specified period of time? Are the limitations of the task clear in terms, say, of how much money is available, how much staff time can be used and how much secretarial and reprographic help is to be forthcoming?

Table 6.2 Stages in effective delegation

Plan delegation	Decide what to delegate and to whom. Assess the task and the person. Decide how much training and help required. Plan the briefing or training session. Give sufficient authority to enable the task to be performed.
Delegate the task	Brief and train the member of staff. Define the task and its limits clearly, making sure that your colleague knows what you want her to achieve and the limits of her authority. Make sure that your colleague understands why the task is important and why she is being asked to do it. Give her clear guidance. Present information clearly, in a logical sequence. Check that she understands what she has to do. Do not assume that your instructions have been understood. Build her confidence. Show that you believe she is capable of performing the task successfully. Brief and train her properly for it. Make clear your role after delegation. Inform other colleagues about the delegation of task and authority.
Monitor progress	Do not interfere. Give help when needed. Check success by monitoring from a distance. Monitor results rather than processes.

Second, successful delegation depends on having the authority to carry out the responsibilities. Does the team member have the necessary authority to do the job? Can she sign letters or use the school office or take decisions without referring back to the team leader?

Third, being clear about how performance will be judged. Nobody can ever be expected to take on new responsibilities without making some mistakes, but performance criteria should be agreed and specified at the outset. It is against these criteria that the headteacher, team leader or other person responsible for planning and implementing the process of delegation can check that colleagues are succeeding in the delegated task.

Delegation helps the headteacher or the team leader because colleagues are less likely to come to her for help or information about those tasks which have been delegated. It helps the team or staff member to whom the task has been delegated because telling all relevant colleagues that delegation has taken place is to acknowledge that a named colleague has been given the authority to carry out a particular task. It also helps the rest of the staff to know who has that particular responsibility since they can now turn to the appropriate person for help and advice or with suggestions. It should be remembered, however, that although authority has been delegated, the final responsibility has not. This remains with the team leader or the headteacher. Given the demands on the staff of secondary schools, effective delegation is essential. The communication to the staff team and to the rest of the school is vital for the success of the delegation process, for the effective management of the team, and to the work of the teachers and children within the school. Effective communication is a vital part of delegation as it is of all other management functions in secondary school teams.

ACTIVITIES

1 Identify three targets which you have to achieve next term. Follow the guidelines in Table 6.1 and Figure 6.1.

2 Identify one main task which you carry out at the moment and which might be delegated to an identified member of your team. What criteria have you used? Plan a training programme which would enable you to delegate this task and, after obtaining agreement from your colleague, implement the programme.

Chapter 7

Communication in schools

Communication in schools is an extremely complex topic. A thorough coverage of it would deal with everything from policy-making at senior management level to individual job descriptions for each staff member, taking in the school, departmental and team communication systems along the way. It might include formal and informal interviews with staff, pupils, parents and others and would have to look at types, patterns and the content of communication. It would certainly include a discussion of staff handbooks, handbooks for parents, reports and other communications with the wider community. Such an exhaustive analysis of the topic of communication is beyond our scope here. Instead, it is proposed to examine briefly those factors which will tend to inhibit or facilitate communication within schools and to consider those types of communication which are especially relevant to teachers working together in teams within those schools.

Communication can take a variety of different forms but these can be divided into three main categories:

- verbal, including planned and unplanned discussions, one-to-one encounters, small or large meetings and using telephones or tannoys.
- written, including notes, memos, reports, letters, position papers and notices.
- visual, including posters, diagrams, flow-charts, pictures and photographs.

Each form of communication has its contribution to make to the effective management of teams within schools and to the whole school. An understanding of these different types of communication is essential if we are to help pupils to learn; if we are to make a contribution to our different teams; if we are to influence, persuade, negotiate or bargain; and if we are to provide relevant information in appropriate forms to groups such as governors and parents.

PROBLEMS WITH COMMUNICATION

Problems with communication tend to be associated with four aspects of the process:

- Senders
    Do they have something to communicate?
    Do they really want to share it?
    Do they understand it sufficiently to communicate it?
    Is it expressed clearly from the receiver's point of view?
- Receivers
    Have they interpreted the message accurately?
    Is the message important enough to demand attention?
    Are they able to respond to the message?
    Do they want to respond to the message?
- The method of communicating
    Has the appropriate method been selected?
    Has the appropriate time been chosen?
    Can the message easily be distorted in delivery?
- The purpose or intended outcome of the communication
    Is the purpose clear?
    Are the receivers able to carry out the purpose?
    Will they want to carry out the purpose?
    Are the deadlines realistic?

From the above list it can be seen that almost all communication is about action. It is about initiating action, preventing action or giving or requesting information on which action may be based, either now or in the future. We often, consciously or unconsciously, evaluate the effectiveness of our communication in terms of whether or not action has taken place. Most of our routine and not so routine activity requires us to communicate with others; yet, apart from this vague assessment in terms of actions by others, we tend to be singularly unaware of how our messages are coming across, of how effective we are as communicators. We ignore, all too often, those factors which inhibit communication.

The skills which enabled us, as infants, to attract the necessary attention, as adolescents to cope with the strains of impending adulthood, and as teachers to cope with the daily routine of teaching, are not necessarily those which make us effective members or leaders of staff teams in schools. The fact that we have all been communicators for so long often leads us to forget that we may not be as effective as we or other people might like. Good communication must avoid ambiguity and the possibility of being misunderstood or misinterpreted. It should not generate suspicion or hostility since this leads to a situation in which the content of the communication is frequently ignored because of the feelings which it creates. A pleasant letter is more likely to be effective and productive than an unpleasant one. In spite of our lifelong practice in communicating we need to check that we are communicating effectively. This involves transmitting the communication in the most appropriate form; providing enough information but not too much; ensuring that the intended actions occur and that it is clear who is to take them and by when.

Within a group like a staff team there is often so much that has to be communicated that the tendency is to try to communicate too much at any one time or to communicate in a style which is neither appropriate nor acceptable. As a result colleagues can find themselves being told instead of being consulted or being asked instead of being instructed. The sheer size of some schools can exacerbate this situation when, for example, it has proved impossible to find a team member with whom the leader wishes to discuss a matter. The team leader may then write a short note which, because it is written in haste, is ambiguous, unclear or threatening to the reader, but not intended to be so by the writer. From this, team problems grow.

Team problems which have their roots in poor communication are often the product of our attitude to the process of communication. We often see this as an end in itself rather than as a means to an end. Thus, the well-produced notice, the apt memo or the carefully chosen phrase is regarded as the very epitome of good communication when, in fact, this is far from being the case. Effective communication should be understood as the link between thought and action or behaviour. It is the process of conveying hopes, ideas, intentions or feelings from one person to others. A failure in communication can arise in this process when the action or behaviour which follows the communication is inconsistent with the message contained in that communication. A simple example of this is when a team member fails to comply with a request, or fails to act upon an instruction. Such situations are easy to manage. The situations in which the disjunction between message and action is caused by the sender of the message, the team leader or head-teacher, are far more difficult to identify and to handle.

Where, for example, a team leader has made it clear to her team members that certain tasks will be dealt with by one of the team rather than by herself and then is found to be dealing with one of those tasks rather than referring it to the relevant colleague, how might this be interpreted? The intention might have been nothing but good; for example, to help a colleague known to have a heavy workload. The action of the team leader, however, is clearly inconsistent with the message. Team members may interpret the head of department's action as being inconsistent with the stated policy and may then be reluctant to act in accordance with that policy in the future. Further, such a situation may result in the staff team as a whole refusing to take seriously the head of department's stated intention to delegate responsibility in the future.

Such issues as these have to be confronted as part of the communication process within the team if effective communication is to lead to the desired actions and behaviour. All team members need to be aware of those factors which, unless attended to, will inhibit effective communication (see Table 7.1). In particular, a team leader should be aware of the particular characteristics of those with whom communication is taking place. Any communication should be influenced by such knowledge as well as by the outcome which the communication is intended to produce.

Table 7.1 Are communications effective in your school?

Signals of need to improve	*Focus of attention*
Complaining about a lack of communication or about not receiving information.	Examine basis for complaint: it may be valid or it may be caused by frustration or lack of security.
Flourishing grapevine of rumour (often inaccurate) regarding the state of the school and plans for the future.	Unofficial communication channels flourish when formal ones are weak or in times of uncertainty: examine the existing channels of communication.
Confusion about responsibilities among colleagues.	Spell out each person's duties and authority clearly on paper as part of a job description.
Failure to bring major problems to your attention soon enough.	Examine your relationship with colleagues. Do you encourage them to ask for help? Have you spelled out what they should discuss with you before taking action?
Not doing things even though they have been told.	Always follow up communications to check they are carried out.
Making silly mistakes, despite clear instructions.	Are you using two-way communications? Are you checking that they understand and that they can do it? Are you following up to check that appropriate actions are taken?
Not coming forward with ideas for improvement, and show little initiative.	Are you keeping colleagues fully in the picture? Are you trying to build commitment?
Appearing to get the wrong message.	Are you sure that you are communicating clearly, simply and in the most appropriate way?

MAKING COMMUNICATION WORK

Both the sender and the receiver of the communication should be clear about what the objective of the communication is: whether this is to inform, request information, produce action or prevent action. The required outcome of the communication should also be quite unambiguous. The team leader, in sending the communication, needs to be clear about how best to gain the outcome which she is requiring from those to whom the communication is being sent. At the same time the team leader has to bear in mind how frequently communications are issued on this and other matters. The more 'noise' there is in any school or in any staff team caused by frequent communications which to the recipients seem unimportant and trivial, then the more chance there is of any one item of communication, however important, actually getting lost.

Effective communication demands that the message is clear, unambiguous, short and simple. It must be transmitted in a style that is acceptable and understandable. The actions which it may demand should be, as far as possible, easy to understand and easy to execute. The team leader should show concern for those team members with whom she is communicating as well as consistency in the process of communicating. Simple communications can be made to work by following the guidelines set out in Table 7.2.

All communication will be more effective if all the staff of the school recognise that they have a responsibility to ensure that the system works. This means that they play their part by reading notices, opening letters, checking pigeon holes and providing feedback when requested. It also

Table 7.2 Making communication work

Why?	The basic reason for communication is to get someone else to do something.
What?	Spell out exactly what the receiver is to do. Making the messages precise and to the point saves time (and money, if using the telephone).
Who?	When something has to be done tell the person who has responsibility for it and make sure that everyone affected by it is told.
When?	If there is a message for someone it is usually best to tell her now. Putting off communications can result in forgetting, or in a build-up of work. If there is a deadline a reminder can be given at the right time.
How?	Choose the simplest and most direct method to communicate.
Check	Check that the other person grasps what she has to do. Check that it has been done.

means that where the system does not work or is manifestly seen to be inappropriate – not enough or too much information being received or information being received at the wrong time, for example – then they draw this to the attention of the person responsible in a courteous and professional way. Communication in schools and teams can always be improved. A good way to start this is by asking staff to describe existing practices. This enables them to begin to evaluate the communication system within the school and to make suggestions for upgrading it. In this way agreed routines could be established. Everyone can make communication more effective by bearing the following questions in mind:

- What am I trying to communicate? What is the purpose of my communication?
- What are my objectives? What is the nature of the communication? Is the method chosen appropriate for the people receiving the communication?
- Who is it for? Do they need to know? Are they the most appropriate people to receive the communication?
- How should I communicate? Which method or combination of methods should I use? What style can I adopt that is best suited to my target audience?
- When should I communicate? Is one particular time better than any other?
- Where – to what address or location – am I sending this communication?
- If it is written, how do I check that the message has been received?
- Have I established controls to get feedback on whether the message has been correctly received and acted upon?

FORMS OF COMMUNICATION

The general points made in Table 7.2 on how to make communication work can apply to all forms of planned communication. Body language, gesture and unintentional signs and signals are another matter. These are very difficult to control and are open to a range of different interpretations. For example, if somebody looks down during a conversation this in some cultures may indicate submissiveness, disagreement or thoughtfulness, but in other cultures be simply indicative of politeness. Most people find body language difficult to control. Table 7.3 might enable you to recognise non-verbal signals and to recognise some of your own. Remember, however, that to concentrate too much on it can distract attention from other, perhaps far more significant, aspects of effective communication.

In essence a team leader communicates effectively if her message is clear, if it is interpreted as she intended and if it is understood and acted upon. There are some more specific guidelines that can help to improve particular forms of communication. The rest of this chapter will be devoted to looking at ways of making verbal and written communication more effective.

Table 7.3 Body language

Responsive/friendly	*Unresponsive/aggressive*
Smile	Set mouth, face
Nod	Staring
Open-handed gesture	Abrupt movement or speech
Relaxed posture	Keeps distance
Eye contact	Looks beyond you
Relaxed tone of voice	Harsh tone of voice
Controlling/dominating	*Nervous/submissive*
Points	Nervous hand movements
Leans forward	Looks down
Interrupts	Allows interruptions
Ignores responses	Hesitates
Loud, rapid speech	Speaks quietly
Controlling tone of voice	Soft tone of voice

Face-to-face communication

Much of the communication that goes on in school is spoken rather than written. It may be informal, as in a brief discussion of a professional matter, or formal, as in a pre-arranged and planned discussion or in a team meeting. It may be planned or unplanned. It may be long or short. It may involve two or three colleagues or a much larger number. This part of the discussion on communication will concentrate on those areas of verbal communication that involve a small number – two or at most three people – in a discussion that is intended to have a precise outcome and that involves persuasion, negotiation or influencing. This type of communication is different from, and not a substitute for written communication. There are a number of general points that can improve its effectiveness. Always be prepared for such meetings, use questioning techniques to check understanding and move the discussion on, communicate clearly, listen accurately and build agreement. In order to do this:

Prepare
- Define your own aim clearly.
- Predict the other person's aim, and whether he or she might shift to a point of compromise.
- Prepare your case, collecting any information you need.
- Predict major objections the other person may raise.
- Decide how you can best overcome each objection.

Question

- Use closed questions to check facts:
  How many pupils did you take?
  What is the date of the next meeting?
  Precisely when did it happen?
- Use open questions to encourage others to talk, explain or put a point of view:
  Can you tell me what has happened?
  What are your feelings about . . . ?
  How do you think we should tackle . . . ?
- Use probing or reflecting questions to explore a point further or to check understanding:
  What changes have you noticed since . . . ?
  What makes you say that?
  How do you know?
- Avoid using leading questions.
- Avoid a series of questions.
- Avoid jumping in too quickly.

Listen

- Do not interrupt. Let the other person finish speaking (unless he or she is straying too far from the point). Interrupting will only irritate.
- Concentrate. Listen carefully to what is being said. Keep your mind clear – do not think about your next point, or you will miss what is being said.
- Hear what is said. It is a common mistake to 'half listen', hearing what you want to hear, rather than what is actually said.
- Note key points. Mentally summarise the most important points that the other person makes. It is often a good idea to start your reply by restating these key points.
- Be objective. Do not let your interpretation be distorted by your opinion or feelings about the other person, by his or her appearance or the way he or she speaks.
- Evaluate. Weigh up what she is saying. Ask yourself 'Am I getting the complete picture?' Does what she is saying support or alter the aim?
- Decide the real meaning. Sometimes you have to look beyond the words themselves to get it. Points omitted, tone of voice, manner and facial expression can all provide added meaning.

Communicate

- Present your case, keeping it short and sharp. Use only a few strong facts, expressed in the way that will make most impact.

- Put it across with confidence, emphasising essential points to hold the other person's attention.
- Listen carefully to what the other person says, look for objections and opportunities for agreement.
- Choose the most persuasive way to respond to any objection. Objections often arise as a result of misunderstandings. If this is the case, clarify the nature of the misunderstanding and answer it. If the objections raise new information or ideas, you may modify your own approach to reach agreement.
- Question frequently to clarify points, to check progress, and to get the other person to build on your case.

Agree

- Bargain to reach agreement, trading any shift you make for an equivalent shift by the other person.
- Watch for signals that the other person is ready to agree a deal.
- Close the deal speedily, spelling out what has been agreed so that there is no misunderstanding.

If a team leader can prepare herself in this way for a discussion with an individual colleague or with a small group then she will find that these planned, semi-formal, face-to-face encounters become even more productive. The following sequence, which can be adapted to suit a number of different circumstances, can also help to give a structure to such discussions.

Set atmosphere

- friendly greeting.
- comfortable seating.
- settling-in 'small talk'.

Start discussion

- establish purpose and length of discussion.
- explore the situation as they see it.
- what is your interpretation?

Listen

- be attentive.
- make brief notes of key points.
- do not evaluate yet.
- listen to what is said and what is omitted.

Clarify

- check your understanding.
- use reflecting-back or probing techniques.

Make proposals

- ensure compatibility with existing attitudes or satisfaction of needs or solution of problem.
- emphasise least controversial aspects.
- show similarity with other people – do not make them feel unusual – but make solution unique to this situation.
- build agreements.

Discover feelings about proposals

- direct question ('How do you feel about . . . ?').
- List objections (itemise each one).
- clarify ('Do you mean . . . ?').
- summarise when you feel you have them all ('Are these your concerns . . . ?').
- try to get to 'yes'.

Look at solutions together

- 'How can we tackle . . . . .?' (each one).
- check off against list of concerns.
- get agreement as frequently as possible.
- deal with areas of agreement first, then tackle any areas of disagreement.

Agree actions

- 'I will do . . . '.
- 'Can you do . . . ?'.
- establish follow-up methods and time-scale.

Follow-up

- make sure you do what you promised.
- make sure they do what they promised.
- make sure solutions are applied and work.

In this sequence the single most important stage is that of listening. When we are seeking to influence colleagues or when we are bargaining or negotiating with them we should spend much more time listening than talking. A good indication is that an effective negotiator will listen for about 80 per cent of the time and talk for only 20 per cent. The more we are able to listen to others, the more we will be able to communicate with them and they with us. If a team member believes that the views which she expresses to the team leader are received in a positive, receptive way the communication is likely to succeed. This does not mean that people have to agree with each other, but it does mean that team leaders have to devise their own listening style. The listener should adopt a style which shows that she is concentrating on what is being said to her and which encourages the team member to talk, rather than a style which creates opportunities for the team leader to express her own views. Listening has to be an active and not a passive process which involves the listener in checking that she has understood what is being said and that there is a clear agreement at the end of the conversation on what will happen as a result of it. This should not be left to chance and should be clearly understood by both parties at the end of the discussion. Active listening, then, leads to effective communication.

This is not to say that all communication between team members is or should be verbal communication or individual discussions. This form of communication does have its advantages because it provides opportunity for immediate feedback and for the modification of the message if this is necessary. It also indicates if the message is as clear and unambiguous to the team members as it is to the team leader who may know much more of the background than her colleagues. Thus, it can provide the opportunity for team members to ask questions and to allow feelings to be displayed and expressed more fully, especially in a non-verbal way. Oral communication is, however, expensive on time. It should, therefore, be used when the matter under consideration is complex or emotive, unpleasant or even personal. It should also be used to give praise or where the issue is particularly important. Remember, however, that it may be necessary to record what is said in some way. This should be agreed beforehand and confirmed by sharing the record afterwards. Many team leaders feel more confident when they are communicating in writing.

Written communication

All forms of written communication have their place in the workings of the school team, but in order to be effective they have to be read and understood. It is more difficult to detect errors and ambiguities in the receiving of written communications. The appropriate phrase or sentence can be chosen to convey just the right idea. It is important to ensure that this is what happens and to prevent meanings from being obscured. For example, the use of long words when shorter ones will do may lead to ambiguity. So may employing phrases which pad out the writing.

Some phrases have almost become jargon in the sense that they are intended as a shorthand to convey meanings but, in fact, do not do this. Phrases like 'after mature reflection' which normally means 'I have changed my mind', or 'you were right and I was wrong', and 'it is the consensus of the meeting' which may mean either 'we agree' or 'I am not sure what we have agreed but I am going to interpret it my way' tend to obscure meaning. The tendency to use several words when one would be adequate, and probably much clearer, has a similar effect.

Memos and letters for distribution inside schools need to be as carefully written as those communications going to people outside. Ideally such written communications should be no longer than one side of A4 paper. It should deal with one issue or a small number of closely related issues. It should be clearly addressed to a specific audience. It should make clear to the receiver what it is that the sender expects the receiver to do as a result of receiving the communication and by when. KISS (Keep It Short and Simple) is valuable advice.

Most organisations have their own jargon and shorthand. Schools are no exception. All schools use the jargon that is current in the educational world. Often this takes the form of sets of initials. When such acronyms are used they should be written in full the first time. Schools often develop their own jargon to fit their own particular circumstances. There is nothing wrong with using this provided it is understood by all concerned. Compiling glossaries of terms can help with this, especially for those new to the school community. For example, the precise meaning of module may need explaining within the context of the work of a particular school. Where letters or reports are going to parents, governors or others who may not be familiar with the language of education or the particular circumstances of the school this is particularly important.

In spite of some of the obvious problems with getting it right, written communication has certain advantages and should be used for specific purposes. By its very nature it provides a permanent record of the message, provided that the storage and retrieval system used by the recipient is effective. Thus, it provides a record of agreements, ideas and actions. It can convey complex ideas or directions that might otherwise be difficult to remember. It can be used to pass on detailed and extensive information and give opportunities for detailed and thoughtful responses. Written communication, then, is different from and not a substitute for the spoken word. Where written and oral communication are treated as interchangeable alternatives communication quickly breaks down.

Visual communication

Until recently the main form of visual communication in most schools was the notice board. Notice boards are extremely useful for giving information quickly and simply to relatively large groups of people with little cost. Such notices are only effective if people get into the habit of looking at notice boards frequently, say every morning and/or lunch-time. Team leaders can help to encourage this habit in a number of ways. If notice boards are used regularly colleagues will be encouraged to look at them. If team members know that urgent notices will be placed on a given notice board at specific times they are more likely to look at it. Colour coding of different types of notices can help team members to see from a distance if a particular kind of notice has recently been displayed. Above all, if notice boards are well organised, and if out-of-date notices are removed, then communication through notice boards will be effective. Somebody in each team should have the responsibility for this simple but important task.

Schools are now making more use of other forms of visual display. Some are producing their own promotional videos. Now that media studies is taught in many schools, making such videos is not as costly or difficult as it once was. The new forms of assessment associated with the National Curriculum require examples of pupils' work to be kept. Video cameras are used for this in a growing number of schools. The advantage of using video cameras, or the cheaper and equally effective camcorders which combine a camera and video recorder, is that developments over time can be shown and processes as well as outcomes recorded.

At a simpler level, commercially produced or purpose built timetabling boards with a complex range of signs and symbols designating subjects, teachers, classes and rooms tend to be a familiar sight in schools. Similar but less complex boards can be used by teams to plan the use of facilities such as specific teaching spaces, items of equipment such as televisions or computers, resource collections or sets of books. Similarly some form of visual display can be useful to the headteacher or team leader as an aid to planning and using time effectively. A diagram indicating when all the major routine tasks have to be completed can help to co-ordinate activities across the team. It can show by when certain key tasks have to be completed, indicate where chasing or checking might be required and reveal where insufficient time has been allowed or where likely hold-ups may occur. These may then be dealt with in advance in order to try to prevent them happening. If the diagram includes a space in which to indicate when each stage has been completed it can be even more useful to the team leader. This technique can be applied to the planning and implementation of almost all routine and many non-routine activities involving team members and taking place over a relatively long period of time.

Managing meetings

Meetings are an extremely common form of communication at both school and team level. Indeed, meetings are intended to be an integral part of the communication process in schools but many of them fail in this intent. Some meetings may be small, perhaps a working party of a few colleagues from a larger team. Some will involve all team members while others may involve the whole of the school staff. To run a meeting effectively, whatever its size, the person responsible for it needs to be clear about its purpose. Successful meetings are those which are productive and are not regarded by those attending them as a waste of time. Many meetings take place in directed time. They have a precise and limited duration. Time must therefore be used effectively. Many more meetings are held in twilight hours when people are tired and not at their most effective. These meetings must be well organised to get the best out of those who attend them and to justify the expenditure of time by those people at the meeting. Having an agreed finishing time for all meetings is good because it removes one of the uncertainties from attending meetings. Nothing destroys enthusiasm for meetings more quickly than the meeting which has no end. Equally, nothing is more likely to undermine an important item on a staff meeting agenda than introducing it too late in the meeting so that lack of time precludes proper discussion. It is even more inept to introduce such an item and then interrupt discussion and postpone it to the next meeting. Careful agenda planning is essential. Important and regular meetings ought now to be scheduled so that everyone knows in advance when staff meetings, year meetings, curriculum team meetings and other similar meetings will be held throughout the school year. This does not preclude the possibility of calling extra meetings, of cancelling meetings when there is no business, of arranging different meetings.

Advanced warning and a regular, known sequence help to ensure that the appropriate people attend the meeting. This, in turn, minimises the possibility of somebody not knowing about decisions which have been taken or the preparation necessary for the next meeting. A minutes secretary will be necessary to record those decisions and the actions which have to be taken before the next meeting. This record will go some way to avoid the irritating processes, for those who did attend, of explaining to a non-attender what happened last time. The published schedule of meetings might indicate who is expected to attend particular meetings although in small schools this may well be self-evident. The most significant factor in encouraging colleagues to spend time in meetings is the organisation of those meetings. If the meeting is perceived to be useful then teachers will attend it.

Every fruitful meeting has to be planned. Planning starts with a decision about what the real point of the meeting is to be. What sort of meeting is it and what is to be achieved? Meetings can, of course, be defined in terms of their membership: for example, a year group meeting or a curriculum team meeting. Alternatively, a meeting might be defined in terms of its frequency as with the weekly, monthly or termly meeting. Such designations give an indication of the timing and the membership of the meeting but they still tell us little about the purpose and function of the meeting. In most cases this is because meetings tend to serve a variety of different functions and, because of this, they tend to be too long and relatively confused affairs at which miscommunication is more common than illumination because those attending do not recognise when the meeting has changed from one type to another. There is nothing wrong with holding multi-purpose meetings provided that the chairperson and the others at the meeting are clear exactly what function they are being asked to carry out at any one time (see Table 7.4).

A meeting is often called to give information. The staff team may be briefed about changes in school policy, brought up-to-date on current events

---

Table 7.4 Purposes of meetings

Below are different purposes – a meeting may be concerned with one of these purposes only, or the different items of the meeting agenda could have different purposes.

Putting information across	You want the group to grasp information.
Obtaining information	You want information for yourself or for other colleagues – either hard facts or opinions.
Persuading	You want to negotiate with the group.
Solving a problem	You want to generate and examine a number of possible solutions to a problem.
Making a decision	You want the group to reach a conclusion on a particular issue.
Instructing	You want the group to grasp and be able to apply certain skills or knowledge.
Motivating	You want the group to be committed to a particular course of action.

---

or told about particular arrangements. These briefing or advice meetings depend heavily on the team leader, or whoever is chairing the meeting. She has to be fully informed and in control of the information which she wishes to impart, as well as able to deal with relevant questions while, at the same time, not being sidetracked by irrelevant ones. Some thought needs to be given to providing information before the meeting since it is a waste of everyone's time to hold up a meeting while people digest material which could have been given to them well in advance. Similarly some information can best be presented on an OHP rather than by word of mouth. This is usually true of numerical data such as intake figures or class sizes.

A related form of meeting is the one called to seek information or to test opinions; although it might be asked if meetings are the most effective way of doing this. All too often people arrive at such meetings unsure about its precise purpose. They expect to be able to take a decision, rather than to provide information on which decision-making might be based. It is very easy to move from seeking information about a topic to taking decisions about it if the meeting is not chaired carefully and sensitively. It is particularly important that those organising such meetings are clear in their own mind about the nature of the meeting and that they remain so throughout the meeting, guiding its progress firmly.

A third common form of meeting is the persuading or influencing meeting. This takes place when a specific course of action has been decided upon and the team has to be convinced that this is the most appropriate way forward: for example, a team considering a new way of recording pupils' progress where the actual decision to use a particular approach has already been taken, but where the team leader wants agreement on this particular form of the record. It should not be confused with a meeting at which decisions are to be argued through. In this type of meeting the onus is again on the team leader to be fully informed and to be able to present information concisely and clearly. More is required, however, than a simple summary of information. The team leader may need, for example, to outline the present situation and indicate what the problems are and then to show how the new proposals will meet those deficiencies before asking team members to comment on the proposals. She may also need to negotiate some conditions or compromises, such as over the length of time allowed for implementation. These meetings can often become debates although their main purpose is to influence.

Some meetings are called specifically to solve problems. They may use a technique similar to brainstorming or simply use general discussion to generate a number of alternative solutions to the problem under consideration. At least, it is to be hoped that a number of solutions will be examined, since there is never a guarantee that the first solution will be the best or that it will be acceptable to all concerned, as we argued previously. Recommendations do, however, need to be made although it is quite proper for a problem-solving meeting to suggest a small number of possible alternatives and to give advice about the advantages and disadvantages of the various possibilities. At the start of the meeting the team leader needs to present the problem clearly. She then has to structure the discussion in such a way as to allow everyone to make contributions, since it is not necessarily those who shout loudest who can offer the most appropriate solutions or the best ideas.

At other meetings the main aim is to reach a decision on a particular matter. Often decision-making meetings are confused with other types of meetings. Those who attend are not sure about the extent to which they are being informed about a decision after it has been taken, consulted about it before it is made, or are, in fact, being asked to make the decision during that meeting. Where a meeting has to reach a decision the team leader should make this clear from the very beginning. It should also be made clear how any decision will be made. This may be done by a majority vote of all those present at the meeting or, at the other extreme, it may be done entirely by the team leader after 'getting a feel of the meeting'. Ideally, of course, the team leader should seek to obtain a consensus of all team members. When the decision is finally reached it should also be announced in such a way as to leave no doubt in the minds of those present about what has been decided.

The main purpose of some meetings is to instruct. This usually occurs in the context of staff development or in-service training where a group of teachers is being shown how to use an item of equipment or a new curriculum package. This is a meeting, just like any other, and it will need similar preparation if it is to be successful. Motivating meetings are less common, although they do take place. They are intended to obtain commitment from a group of staff to a particular course of action and to generate enthusiasm for it rather than a mere acceptance which may be the outcome of the persuading meeting. They are similar in kind, but differ in degree.

Organising meetings

Knowing how any meeting is to proceed is helped by understanding what type of meeting it is and by being aware of the intended outcome. Team members need to know in advance whether, for example, it is a briefing meeting or a problem-solving meeting. Much time can be saved by ensuring that the objectives of the meeting are clear and by distributing brief but relevant discussion papers well before the meeting is due to take place. By reading and discussing such papers before the meeting many ambiguities and misunderstandings can be sorted out in advance. This helps to prevent valuable time being wasted during the meeting clarifying points which could just as easily have been sorted out beforehand. The team leader may also wish to spend some time before the meeting discussing each item with colleagues, exploring alternatives, consolidating a point of view and ensuring that those who are leading on any particular item are prepared for it. Communication about the business of the meeting in advance is a vital part of planning an effective meeting, not least because it enables the team leader to inform everybody about the objectives of the meeting before it takes place. It also enables the team leader to know who may be attending and to have some idea of the size of the group.

The size of the group is important because the number of people in a meeting is an important factor in determining how far it is possible to gain the maximum benefit from using meetings as a form of communication. Benefit is assumed but not often made explicit. Once we understand its advantages we can begin to ensure that our meetings are conducted so that the maximum benefit is obtained from them. In a meeting everyone attending receives more or less the same message at the same time. It is possible, in fairly small meetings, to check everyone's grasp of that message immediately. Reactions can be heard and observed, and queries or difficulties may be resolved during the meeting. Often problems can be solved and decisions made collectively. These processes, taken together, can contribute towards building a team identity and encouraging the group to work together.

Group size is also important because there is a limit to how far it is possible to communicate with larger numbers of people. In large groups it is very difficult to take decisions but fairly easy to brief staff. It is also necessary to have the furniture for the meeting set out in an appropriate way. It is, for example, no accident that in the House of Commons the opposing groups sit opposite each other and that the business is conducted on the basis of advocacy and debate with very little agreement actually being reached. If a meeting is arranged in a similar way, with potential adversaries facing each other across a table, then it is likely that conflict will ensue. It is far more difficult to have a heated argument with the person seated beside you. Apart from that, some consideration has to be given to how the communication is to flow during the meeting. A circle helps to encourage the sharing of ideas between members of the group, but it is less effective for giving information. Alternatively, by chairing the meeting from a position in front of a semi-circle, information and ideas are more likely to flow to and from the chairperson and not between members of the team. This might, for example, be appropriate for a briefing meeting while the group round the table might be more effective if decisions have to be taken.

The room should be prepared well before the meeting; an essential factor whatever the setting. Visual aids and equipment have to be set up and checked. Nothing destroys the atmosphere of a meeting more quickly than an overhead projector which fails to project, a screen which collapses or invisible visual aids. For a well conducted meeting it is best to have all this ready before colleagues start arriving. Business-like meetings may require colleagues to take notes, so writing materials should be available. In some meetings points of agreement can often be displayed to advantage on a flip chart. The paper can then be displayed in the room or returned to in subsequent discussions. This is especially useful in problem-solving or decision-making meetings.

An agenda should be published giving the starting time, place and finishing time as well as a list of the topics to be covered and the order in which they will be taken. The agenda ought also to state clearly the purpose of the meeting, indicate who is to introduce each topic and which papers relate to each topic. If a meeting includes a number of items with different purposes – giving information, seeking opinion and making a decision for example – then these purposes should be indicated on the agenda to avoid confusion and to save time. An item of information might be listed as 'To receive information on LEA arrangements for allocating the five in-service days' (Mrs Welton). An opinion-seeking item might be worded as 'To consider three mathematics schemes for use in Oakfields Comprehensive School' (Mrs Green). A decision-making item could be introduced as 'To decide on the content of the first in-service day on multicultural education' (Mr Jowett and Ms Gill).

The sequence of items on the agenda also requires some thought. It might be appropriate always to start the meeting by looking at the minutes from the previous meeting to give team members an opportunity under 'matters arising' to comment or to ask about decisions and actions taken as a result of the last meeting. Informational or briefing items should come before items for discussion or decision in order that the situation can be avoided in which discussion depends on information which the group has not yet been given. Items of business not included on the formal agenda should either come at the end as 'any other business' or there should be an agreed procedure for including such items on the agenda. If colleagues are to prepare in advance for meetings, items of other business should be strictly limited. Perhaps such items might be restricted to early warnings of information to be provided. This opportunity should also be used to remind colleagues of the date, time and place of the next meeting or to arrange this if it is necessary. Items for the agenda should then be submitted at least a week before the next meeting together with an indication of whether they are short items or major business items so that sufficient time can be allocated when planning the meeting. Such an agenda goes a long way towards providing clear ground rules and an appropriate structure for meetings.

If meetings are to contribute to the development of the staff team, especially in a collegiate environment, then it is important that the business is not all conducted by the chairperson or by the most experienced member of staff present. In order to prevent this, team members can and should prepare themselves in advance for the meetings which they attend. At the very least this should mean that they have read all the papers and have at their disposal any information which may be required. If they are to make a formal contribution to an agenda item then this needs to be prepared carefully. The argument should be clear and simple, but accurate and complete. Visual aids often help to get across a complex argument like the significant differences between three mathematics schemes which can more easily be presented as a diagram than as a speech. All colleagues should be clear from the outset about the aims of the meeting and what it has to achieve. If they are not, then they should ask. The aims must be kept in mind throughout the meeting and all contributions should move towards them. In short everyone attending the meeting should accept part of the responsibility for making the meeting work.

The heaviest burden of responsibility for making the meeting work falls on the person in the chair. She has to prepare well in advance. She may wish to ensure that certain alternatives are, at least, considered if not accepted. She may need to prepare her arguments in order to make this happen. Above all the chairperson must allow the discussion to flow. She can encourage this by prompting and asking questions or by injecting ideas. She can bring into the discussion the quieter members of the team. The chairperson can encourage participation by posing questions to the group as a whole, which is less threatening than asking unprepared individuals. This can be supplemented by approaching specific individuals who have been warned before the meeting that this might happen. Open questions to which there are no simple short answers produce more discussion than closed questions with simple answers.

As the meeting progresses the team leader in the chair should summarise and record decisions taken and actions agreed. Where a particular matter appears unclear to the chairperson it should not be ignored or left in the hope that all will become clear at a later stage. Invariably this will not happen. More time will be required to sort out the mess later. If you do not understand what has happened then it is a safe bet that most other people are also confused. The team leader must accept the risk of looking silly, if risk there is, and ask for clarification. She should not proceed until all are clear and have agreed that they understand. Clarifying misunderstandings, seeking further information and indicating what has been decided are all important factors in the successful chairing of meetings. Above all, each item must be concluded clearly, agreements or actions restated and the person responsible for them named. A minutes secretary may be needed for this.

The combination of a well-structured agenda, control from the chair and team members committed to making the meeting work well should ensure that those agenda items which are really important for the work of the team are those which receive the detailed attention, while those which might generate lots of discussion but which are really not all that important are dealt with speedily and effectively. The team might also wish to have a rule about the length of time which must elapse before a decision which it has taken can be reconsidered. This is useful in those situations where strong differences of opinion prevail on a matter which can be tackled in a number of ways, like teaching reading or classroom organisation. It is also the team leader's duty, when conducting the meeting, to avoid the repetition of argument either by the same person or by different people saying the same things. A well-chaired meeting with a good agenda can help with this as well as being an invaluable aid in keeping colleagues to the point.

The secretary and/or the chairperson together should be responsible for recording what happens at the meeting. All that really needs to be recorded is what was decided. If absolutely necessary this can include voting figures but voting should only be used as a last resort. Where an action has been agreed upon, this should also be recorded together with the name of the person responsible for implementing the action and the deadline set for the completion of the task. Minutes should be circulated to all members, including those who were unable to attend the meeting, as soon as possible after the meeting has taken place. Minutes are simply a record of what was decided at a meeting. They are not a detailed account of who said what to whom about which topic.

When the minutes are circulated they should not just go into pigeon holes to be forgotten. It is good practice to highlight tasks that each colleague has agreed to carry out. It may be worthwhile for the team leader to make a note on her own copy of the agenda to follow up some of the points at a later date. Others might also need to be informed of the outcomes of the meeting. The headteacher or deputy may wish to have the minutes as a matter of course. Other colleagues in the school might find them helpful; and, if some

Table 7.5 The organisation of a meeting

Plan	Know the objectives of the meeting and what is to be achieved.
Communicate	Inform other team members what is to be discussed at the meeting and why.
Prepare	Prepare the room and the resources. Put agenda in a sequence and allot appropriate time to each item. Arrange your papers in agenda order. Plan results for each agenda item. Decide location, time, duration and notify all those involved. Prepare yourself and brief those who are to lead the discussion.
Raise points	Declare aims and agenda at outset. Work to agenda sequence, introduce each item in turn. Put across information clearly and confidently.
Manage discussion	Encourage constructive discussion. Keep discussion directed toward aims. Remain in charge throughout. Control the pace of the meeting.
Conclude	At the end of each agenda item present sharp, clear conclusions. Check understanding and acceptance of conclusions.
Report	Prepare a report on all important meetings. Make report short, concise, listing conclusions against each agenda item. If there are agreed follow-up actions, state who does what and when, and who will check.
Follow up	Send out the minutes with highlighted decisions and actions to be taken, by whom and by when. Check that any agreed actions are successfully carried out.

items involve or affect other colleagues, then they ought to receive the minutes as a matter of course. A circulation list for both the agenda and the minutes is always useful. It saves the bother of writing a list or checking each time that you have included everybody. If you keep some spare copies of the minutes you can then always pass one to anyone who has been forgotten for some reason. Smaller schools, with limited secretarial resources, may find that a minute book kept by a member of staff, and then placed in the staffroom, is all that is required. The essential factor is to keep an accurate record of what has been decided and what has to be done, by whom and by when.

Finally it is worth evaluating the meeting itself. Everard and Morris (1985) suggest that we ask the following questions after each meeting and take appropriate action if we are not satisfied with the answer:

- Was the purpose of the meeting clear to all those who attended?
- Was the attendance correct for the subject under discussion? (Who else should have been there? Who was not really needed?)
- Were the participants adequately prepared for the meeting?
- Was time well used?
- How high was the commitment of the participants?
- Did the meeting achieve its purpose?
- What was the quality of the outcome?
- Was there a clear definition of:
    action to be taken following the meeting?
    responsibility for taking the action?
    a mechanism for review of the action?

(Everard and Morris 1985: 52)

Effective meetings are not difficult to organise if they are well planned and if thought is given to the whole process, from deciding what is to be achieved, to circulating an accurate record of what was decided and what actions are to be taken. A team which has its meetings conducted in this way is making good use of its time. It is also more likely to be clear about its overall priorities and how it must set about achieving them. Achieving the priorities of the staff team depends on the effective use of all the time available. This requires that people know how they actually use it. Effective use of time means that how time is being used more and more closely approximates to how time should be used. This has to be determined in the light of the team's own priorities and of those of the school. Ensuring that the total time available to the team is used to greatest effect might mean that tasks are delegated to other members of the team by the team leader or the headteacher. This has to be a careful process involving training and super-vision, as well as the transfer of the appropriate authority to accompany the new responsibilities. Such changes have to be communicated to all staff members. The communication within the team should not be taken for granted. Team leaders especially should be aware of those factors which inhibit good communication as well as knowing which forms of com-munication are appropriate in what circumstances. Taken together these skills will enable the team leader to manage her team in such a way as to ensure that the members can make the maximum contribution to the activities of the school in which they work.

ACTIVITIES

1 Examine the communication process in your school. Can you identify any of the signals listed in Table 7.1? What can you do about them?

2 Over a period of one week analyse all the forms of communication which come to you and leave you. Consider how appropriate and effective each is for its purpose. What changes will you make?

3 Review a representative sample of the meetings you have attended this month. How might the organisation of those meetings be improved in order to make better use of the time you spent attending them? How might your own team meetings be improved?

4 Draw up a full agenda for your next team or staff meeting, and then work through the stages in Table 7.5 to plan and conduct the meeting.

Chapter 8

Curriculum profiles and job descriptions

We have seen that the management and organisation of teams of teachers in secondary schools is an extremely complex matter. Headteachers, team leaders and others with similar responsibilities have to provide a framework within which the aims of the whole school can be translated into objectives and tasks for the different teams within the school. A range of management skills have to be deployed to ensure that the various objectives are achieved. These objectives are themselves subject to continual review and redefinition over time.

In this chapter the emphasis is on how the gathering of information about what teachers actually do as individuals and as members of teams can contribute to the effective management and organisation of those teams and of the whole school. The chapter begins by suggesting another approach to data collection that can complement the school audit or review: the curriculum profile. It then goes on to show how the writing of job descriptions and person specifications can make a valuable contribution to team management in secondary schools.

The central argument in this chapter is that good team management involves making the most effective use of the staff within those teams. Such understanding comes, in part, from teachers knowing their own individual responsibilities and the expectations attached to them. It may also come from being aware of the roles played by colleagues. As Poster (1976) reminds us, an outsider would scarcely believe how often teachers in a school disclaim all knowledge of what colleagues are doing or of what they might reasonably be expected to do. This lack of knowledge is frequently presented as a virtue. It may, however, lead to isolation and parochialism which can make work in schools extremely difficult, especially when much of that work can best be done on a team basis. How far do a school's development plans depend on enabling colleagues to share and develop further the expertise which they undoubtedly have? How can a climate be created in which this understanding and knowledge is made more readily available to all the team members within the school? One way forward might be to begin with a curriculum profile.

THE CURRICULUM PROFILE

The curriculum profile is a technique for identifying what the school is doing at the present time and what else it might still need to do. It helps to show how tasks and responsibilities are allocated and to consider how appropriate the current deployment of staff is. It can help to clarify who is responsible for what, as well as giving an indication of those areas of responsibility which are not being covered. This does not imply that schools need to be rigidly organised or that the demarcations between colleagues have to be inflexible, since there will inevitably be many areas where responsibilities and duties overlap. A curriculum profile should gather information about the total work of the school. A thorough analysis will specify the unique characteristics which differentiate the work of one teacher from another. This will eventually provide a clear picture of all those activities which go to make up the work of any school. It should be remembered that the environment is dynamic and the school must therefore always be changing in order to adapt itself to its environment.

This has never been more important than now as secondary schools engage with the implications of the National Curriculum, especially as it affects them at key stages 3 and 4. Profiling must therefore be a continuous process if it is to enable an examination of how effectively schools as a whole, as well as teams within them, are responding to the demands of curriculum change. A rigorous approach to compiling the curriculum profile, which admittedly is a time-consuming process in the first instance, is invaluable here. It should be the result of a systematic process of collecting and recording. Some possible techniques are outlined in Table 8.1. They combine an analysis of the written evidence concerning what the school is doing with observational and interview evidence which may be more impressionistic. It is important that the whole staff should be involved in this process and that it should be carried out in an open and positive way.

There are three component parts to a full curriculum profile.

- a profile of the individual members of staff;
- an analysis of the school itself;
- an identification of possible areas for future development.

The profiles of individual members of staff are related to their job descriptions but provide more useful information and can be used as a basis for constructing or, by negotiation, modifying job descriptions. The profile contains no evaluative or judgemental content. It is a statement of qualifications, activities and interests. As such it is best compiled either by the teacher herself or in conjunction with a colleague. The headings in Table 8.2 give an indication of what material might be included in such an individual profile, although not every teacher will be involved in every aspect of the work indicated.

Table 8.1 Techniques for producing a curriculum profile

1   Build up a picture of the work from previous profiles, job descriptions, timetables, schemes or work, teachers' records, curriculum documents and other written evidence.
2   Observe the teacher in a variety of different settings within the school over a period of time.
3   Interview the teacher about all aspects of his or her work in the school.
4   Use structured or open-ended questionnaires given to the teacher, head of department, deputy head, headteacher or other relevant person.
5   Employ self-recording of activities in the form of a structured diary but taking into account the different demands at different times.
6   Apply some form of audio or visual recording of a range of teaching and related activities.

The outcome of a complete set of profiles will be, at the very least, a clear indication of the division of responsibility within the school. The profiles may also reveal areas in which efforts are being duplicated or areas which are not being covered at all. In a general way the individual profile should provide a total picture of what a particular teaching position entails whatever the specifics of it might be. The profiling for individual staff might be organised at a departmental level and the results collated by a member of the department. These aggregated results will give a departmental curriculum profile which can then contribute towards that of the whole school.

Care needs to be taken to distinguish between the vital components of a position and those aspects of it which are the consequences of the special interests of the present holder of the post. This information will tend to be either descriptive in the sense that it outlines what a teacher actually does or personal in the sense that it lists qualifications, experience and interests. Methods 1 and 4 in Table 8.1 may be the quickest ways of collecting information from a group of teachers, but those methods may be less reliable and accurate than other methods. Methods 2, 3 and 5 will take more time but may be more accurate. Method 1 is probably the least threatening of all since it concentrates on written documents, while method 3 may be the most necessary in even a small secondary school. Method 6 may be the most costly unless the appropriate equipment is available, but it has the virtue of being very accurate and may be especially useful where teaching takes place in a fairly restricted area – around a forge or a kiln, in a small music room or other specialist area. For the most comprehensive form of individual profile, a selection of all the methods should be used with methods 3, 4 and 5 forming the basis of the analysis. The time and effort devoted to this should be determined by how it is to be used in the school.

Table 8.2 Curriculum profile for individual members of a department

Role in the school
    Title and position.
    To whom responsible.
    For whom responsible.
    For what responsible.
    Copy of personal timetable.

Teaching activities
    Subject expertise, age ranges taught and pastoral work undertaken.
    Procedures used.
    Resources and equipment used.
    Record keeping and self-evaluation techniques.
    Assessment procedures.

Responsibilities and duties
    Planning.
    Administration.
    Staff development.
    Curriculum and assessment.

School responsibilities
    School planning.
    School administration.
    School staff development.
    Curriculum and assessment.

Other activities and responsibilities
    Involvement with clubs and societies.
    Visits, field trips, sporting events.
    Courses attended, other professional activities.
    LEA curriculum planning and development meetings.

Qualifications
    Academic, professional and educational including initial training and further
      qualifications.
    Experience.
    Knowledge, skills and interests.

A further development of the individual profile might be to relate the qualifications and experience part of the profile to the areas of learning and experience listed in *The Curriculum from 5 to 16; Curriculum Matters 2* (DES 1985d: 16). These form the basis of Table 8.3. As can be seen from the table, the individual profile indicates areas in which the individual teacher has qualifications, experience or interest. It will also show whether she has a need or desire to gain some experience or qualifications in any particular area. This approach can then be useful in forward planning, curriculum development and staff development. As *Curriculum Matters 2* reminds us:

Schools need to examine existing practice to establish the extent to which particular topics, aspects and subjects are already contributing to these areas and to the development of knowledge, skills and attitudes. They will then be in a position to decide on any changes and additions which may be required.

(DES 1985d: 16–17)

This table is one way of relating what the staff do to the curriculum as it might be. An approach based on the National Curriculum programmes of study areas would achieve a similar effect.

A similar approach could be adopted for the curriculum profile of the school. It might start with a form which lists the nine curriculum areas across the top and the departments down the left-hand side. If sufficient space is provided it will then be possible to show, by subdividing each of the nine sections, which departments are making a contribution to which areas, which have experience of them, which have an interest in them and which are interested in developing skills in particular areas. This approach can also be adapted to include further curriculum areas which might be of direct concern to the school. In some schools it may be thought appropriate to include other areas of school activity such as assessment, record keeping or staff development. By collecting this information it is possible to build up a picture of what a school is doing across the broad spectrum of its curriculum related activities. This may reveal what is not being done or what is being duplicated. It may lead the staff of a school to focus directly on how well certain areas of experience are taught in the school. Colleagues can explore exactly how far the school provides a curriculum incorporating the areas of experience and the requirements of the National Curriculum. It can help to show how far the curriculum meets the criteria of breadth, balance, relevance and differentiation that are identified in *Curriculum Matters 2* (DES 1985d).

A method of recording this data is to be found in Table 8.4. It must be remembered, however, that the process of recording the information is only a necessary prelude to its analysis and to the professional debate about how well the school is doing. Such a process of discussing the performance of the school in broad terms with reference to the curriculum and to other areas of school life leads naturally into the third aspect of the school profile. As a result of such professional discussions judgements can be made about the strength of the school and about how far it is providing an appropriate curriculum for its pupils, both in terms of the current documents on the curriculum and in relation to the particular situation of the school. It can also be seen from these curriculum profiles where colleagues might like to develop a future interest. In this way the futher development needs of the staff can be taken into account as the development plan for the school is formulated. It is too much to expect that the needs of the school will coincide exactly with the wishes of the staff in this matter; but it is possible to see

Table 8.3 A curriculum related staff profile

	Qualifications		Experience	Interest	Future
	Initial	*INSET*			
Aesthetic and creative					
Human and social					
Linguistic and literary					
Mathematical					
Moral					
Physical					
Scientific					
Technological					
Spiritual					

where the strengths and the gaps might be in what the school is able to provide and to begin to identify ways of filling those gaps. A similar approach can be adopted at team level.

The curriculum profile enables the staff of the school to identify where changes need to be made and where the school needs to improve its performance. It enables those with management responsibility in the school to examine what steps need to be taken to bring about that improvement as well as to consider the resource implications of that process, including the deployment of staff. The object of developing the school is to improve the work of the pupils and it is here that the evidence of the success or otherwise of the school's development must be sought. The means to bringing about this improvement will be, at least in part, staff development. The curriculum profiles, the analysis of the strengths and gaps in the provision which the school is making for its pupils, and the proposed future developments are all part of exploring the existing situation at the team level within the school as well as for the whole school.

JOB DESCRIPTIONS

A further crucial element in the deployment and development of staff in the school is the job description since this provides each teacher with a reference point for her own work in the school. Once the curriculum profiles and the planning for the future have been considered it is necessary to formalise the existing duties and responsibilities for each member of staff in the form of a job description. A job description can reinforce the process embarked upon by the curriculum profile in that it leads to further clarification about who is responsible for what within the school. It should not, however, lead to a rigidity and inflexibility among the staff about how they carry out their professional activities. For all practical purposes, especially when appointing new members of staff, the process of writing a job description can best be understood in two distinct but related parts. These are, first, describing the duties and responsibilities attached to a post and, second, specifying the qualifications, experiences and abilities required to carry out those duties and responsibilities. The first part of this process is variously described as a job description, job specification or some other similar term, whereas the second process is often also called a job specification. This inevitably creates a certain amount of confusion. To avoid this it helps to call the first process a job description and the second a person specification. The job description, therefore, is a description of the duties and responsibilities attached to a post, whilst the person specification is a description of those characteristics for which one would look in somebody fulfilling those duties.

There appears to be broad agreement about what a job description will contain. Everard suggests that it should include:

Table 8.4 A school profile

Section one: Areas of experience

Department	Aesthetic/creative						Human/social						Linguistic						Mathematical						Moral/spiritual						Physical						Scientific/Technological					
	R	Q	E	I	T	FI	R	Q	E	I	T	FI	R	Q	E	I	T	FI	R	Q	E	I	T	FI	R	Q	E	I	T	FI	R	Q	E	I	T	FI	R	Q	E	I	T	FI

Key to columns:
R = Have staff responsible for
Q = Have staff qualified in
E = Have staff experienced in
I = Have staff interested in
T = Have staff with INSET training in
FI = Have staff with future interest in

Table 8.4 Continued

Section two: Other curriculum areas

Department	Multicultural education						Special educational needs						Economic awareness					
	R	Q	E	I	T	FI	R	Q	E	I	T	FI	R	Q	E	I	T	FI

Section three: Other activities

Department	Staff development						Assessment						Library						Relationship with parents					
	R	Q	E	I	T	FI	R	Q	E	I	T	FI	R	Q	E	I	T	FI	R	Q	E	I	T	FI

Key to columns:

R = Have staff responsible for
Q = Have staff qualified in
E = Have staff experienced in
I = Have staff interested in
T = Have staff with INSET training in
FI = Have staff with future interest in

- job title;
- brief description of the purpose of the job;
- reporting relationships;
- description of duties.

(Everard and Morris, 1985: 68)

Lyons and Stenning argue that a job description should record the following facts about the job:

- title of the job;
- indicate to whom the jobholder reports;
- indicate who reports to the jobholder;
- the overall purpose of the job;
- each main function to be carried out by the jobholder;

(Lyons and Stenning 1986: 60)

Dean takes us one stage further when she suggests that the job description should also contain a detailed statement about responsibilities including how far the teacher is responsible for the work of other teachers, ancillary staff, equipment, materials and other activities and facilities (Dean 1985). It is Goodworth, however, who encapsulates the essence of a good job description when he states that it is a detailed description of *what* is to be done (Goodworth 1979).

What does not emerge from such lists of contents for job descriptions, however, is the extent to which the job description must be negotiated with the holder of the post and must match her expectations, especially at the staff selection stage. Nothing is more calculated to be a constant source of conflict and irritation than a significant mismatch between the job description and the teacher's own expectations. The teacher who comes to a school expecting to play a major part in the development and teaching of A level science but who finds that timetable constraints prevent this may, with some justification, become a thorn in the flesh of those who appointed her. The same could be true of a teacher who is presented with a job description which bears only passing resemblance to what she actually does, or which contains some significant changes for which agreement has not been sought. Job descriptions should, therefore, be seen as the property both of the person in the managerial role and of the teacher concerned. The writing of the job description should be based on the actual work which the teacher does and compiled in such a way as to enable that teacher to play a significant part in the process. The final job description should always be agreed with the teacher concerned and should only be changed by agreement on both sides.

Taken together, job descriptions and person specifications must enable structures in schools to be built on the strengths and interests of the staff. Posts should fit people. People should not be made to fit posts. By basing the job description on the postholder's present work, knowledge and skills, development and change is assumed and encouraged. A job description that leaves little or no scope for new ideas and initiatives, inhibits staff development or demands a rigid conformity indicates an inflexible management style which may prove to be totally unacceptable in the current educational climate. Similarly the use of a job description by the postholder to define rigidly the limits of professional activity and involvement would indicate a similarly unhealthy and undesirable approach to education in general and to teaching in particular.

The good job description will concentrate on the what of teaching rather than on the how, although how forms a vital part of job analysis and has a significant place in the person specification. The what-based job description enables the headteacher and the teacher concerned to know both what it is expected will be done and what it is agreed must be done. The job description in Table 8.5 is not untypical yet it is far from adequate. It lists quite specifically the various areas of responsibility under a group of headings. It even includes a statement about minor responsibility. It represents a general agreement about the boundaries of a particular post within school. Yet, in spite of being very specific, it is open to question exactly what the major areas of responsibility are and which areas are less crucial to that position in

---

Table 8.5 Job description

Title   Deputy Head

Role   To assist the headteacher in the efficient running of the school, and to deputise for the headteacher when appropriate.

Responsibility   To the headteacher.

Areas of Concern

(a) *Management*

To be aware of school routine and share responsibility for the smooth running of each day.

To share with the headteacher the responsibility for ensuring that the school's aims and objectives are achieved.

To share in the policy decisions which effect the efficient running of the school.

To help with financial management.

To give practical help and encouragement to any teacher, especially a new colleague.

(b) *Administration*

To share the routine administrative tasks, and to be able to take responsibility for LEA forms, including requisition forms, accident book, registration of pupils, building maintenance forms, school meals forms.

Table 8.5 Job description – continued

(c) *Organisation*

To organise the staff playground duty rota.

To be aware of the health and safety regulations and to promote a safe environment within the school.

To be responsible for internal communication.

To share in the organisation of school events.

To assist the headteacher in setting and maintaining a high standard of behaviour throughout the school.

(d) *Curriculum*

To take teaching responsibility for Physics, formulating aims and objectives with colleagues and producing a scheme of work designed to assist teachers to fulfil the agreed aims and objectives.

To help in the evaluation of the work of the school.

To help maintain high standards of presentation and display of children's work throughout the school and to organise corridor displays.

To share with the headteacher in the professional development of colleagues.

To help welcome all visitors to the school.

(e) *Relationships*

To help support and encourage all teaching and non-teaching staff in the school.

To help promote a happy atmosphere between children and staff.

To assist the headteacher with the effective organisation of parental involvement in the life of the school.

To assist the headteacher in fostering good relationships within the local community.

(f) *Minor Responsibility*

To keep up to date with the latest developments in science by attending relevant courses, reviewing new publications and evaluating new resource materials available.

Agreed

. . . .
Deputy Headteacher

. . . .
Headteacher

Dated

. . . .

the school. Words such as 'share' and 'help with' are not sufficiently indicative of actual responsibility. No clear idea of the boundaries of involvement or the extent of decision-making is given, thus providing every opportunity for the denial of accountability. Under curriculum, the roles given may undermine the authority of another senior colleague, namely, the head of science. A member of the senior management team must be seen to be an integral part of the relevant team as far as her teaching duties are concerned. This example might be improved if it was to be rewritten using the headings in the job description section of Table 8.6. An effective job description will contain all the information subsumed under those headings.

The revised job description makes it clear exactly what the main function is: to assist the headteacher in the effective running of the school. It then indicates how this will be done in terms of what the particular contributions will be. These can, of course, be changed over time but the implication of this particular job description is that the development and implementation of a successful LMS policy will be one of the four major duties of this deputy. The others are liaising with feeder primary schools, staff development and teaching A level physics. The administration of LMS for the school will involve working with governors as well as with teacher colleagues. The other significant addition to the material in Table 8.6 is the various attempts which have now been made to describe exactly what is to be done. For example, the number of meetings with the relevant staff of the primary schools is indicated.

The deadline for producing the first set of LMS guidelines is indicated and the frequency of PTA meetings is shown. This is to avoid the creation of unrealistic and open-ended commitments for the postholder and to clarify the expectations about what has to be done and by when. The use of words like 'organise', 'plan' and 'attend' help to keep the statement of duties concise. If there is to be clarity and precision each duty description should seldom be of more than fifteen words.

If a job description is to be really useful it must be kept short, probably concise enough to fit on one side of A4 paper. It is vital to remember that a job description is a device which helps to spell out exactly what is expected of the teachers. It is not meant to be a method of establishing demarcation between people and jobs in the everyday running of the school. It is a method of helping headteachers and other colleagues to consider the type of person who should be appointed, as a basis for the regular development of teachers. It is also a way of clarifying the role of each member of staff. Everybody knows what the work of a deputy headteacher involves until some dispute arises about who is responsible for what and when. Most of the time the central duties are reasonably clear but additional or peripheral duties are often negotiated by individuals and become traditional in a school. In our example the membership of the PTA committee is one such situation. Similarly the number and frequency of important meetings should

Table 8.6 A job description and specification for a secondary school deputy
headteacher

Job Description

Job title
Deputy headteacher

Responsible to
The headteacher

Main function
To assist the headteacher in
achieving the aims and objectives of
the school and to act as head of the
school in the absence of the head
teacher

Main duties
To develop a policy for local
financial management of the school.
To produce guidelines for all staff
by the end of the next academic
year.
To plan INSET courses on LMS for
all staff.
To organise, in conjunction with the
headteacher, the induction of new
colleagues.
To be responsible for the integration
of new colleagues into the staff team.
To plan effective liaison with the four
linked primary schools and to
organise at least two meetings a
year with the staff of the primary
schools who are responsible for
pupil transfers.
To organise duty lists on a termly
basis and to amend them daily as
required.
To attend the termly meetings of the
PTA committee as a staff member.
To teach A level physics.
To ensure that the school's budget
is effectively managed.
To provide for the professional
development of colleagues.

Person Specification

Job title
Deputy headteacher

Qualifications
Qualified teacher status with
emphasis on secondary education.
A good honours degree in physics or
related area.
Evidence of attending courses in
school management and in financial
management.

Experience
Evidence of experience in managing
school finance.
Evidence of working with school
governors.
At least four years as a head of
department.
Evidence of experience in
co-ordinating the work of colleagues.
Evidence of experience in controlling
stock.
Evidence of experience in helping
with the professional development of
colleagues.
At least ten years as teacher in a
secondary school.
Recent experience of teaching
A level physics.

Aptitudes
Evidence of successful class
teaching.
Evidence of successful departmental
management and organisation.
Evidence of ability to work with
colleagues, especially newly
appointed members of staff.
Evidence of ability to organise
school-based in-service courses.

Table 8.6 Continued

To share in policy decisions which affect the efficient running of the school. To ensure that the routine administration of the school functions effectively.

Responsible for
Carrying out main duties.
Ensuring that main responsibilities are carried out.
The work of [list the names of all those who work to and report to this deputy. The list will include the colleague modifying the computer program and the secretary mentioned below].

Resources
Fifteen hours non-contact time each week.
The assistance of a colleague for the equivalent of three hours a week to install and modify the LMS computer program.
£400 annually from capitation for three years.
The equivalent of two days of secretarial time each week from the LMS secretary.

Evidence of ability to communicate successfully with pupils across the secondary age and ability range.
Evidence of ability to work successfully with colleagues in other schools.
Evidence of organisational and administrative ability.
Evidence of ability to work positively with colleagues.

Physical
Must pass LEA medical.

Interests
Evidence of interest in team sports.
Must have current driving licence to drive minibus.
Evidence of interest in computers would be an advantage.

---

also be specified. Since teaching is, by its very nature, dynamic then job descriptions need to be reviewed regularly. The description and its underlying perceptions will change over time. These changes need to be detected, discussed and recorded with the co-operation and agreement of the postholder to ensure that colleagues are clear about the what of each post within the school.

PERSON SPECIFICATION

If job descriptions are about the what of a job then person specifications are about the who of it. On the basis of a person specification it should be possible to identify what kind of person might be best able to fulfil the requirements of the described post. Broadly speaking, therefore, the person specification describes not the post itself but the person who is required to fill it or, in the case of an existing postholder, the abilities which the postholder ought to have or ought to be developing. It is patently unfair to appoint a candidate to a post for which she was clearly not qualified; but it is often forgotten by headteachers, inspectors and governors, who are under considerable pressure to ensure that the work of the school can continue in spite of staffing difficulties, that it is no less unfair to expect a teacher to teach an unfamiliar subject without adequate time for preparation and/or re-training and the provision of suitable extra support. The particular attributes and skills necessary to perform the job effectively should be made explicit, if only to act as an indication of where training and development are necessary. Thus, the specification for the existing postholder should show what qualities and experience she brings to bear on the work being done. It should also give some indication of areas for future thought and develop-ment to enable performance to be improved, promotion prospects to be enhanced and the needs of the school more fully met. As with the job description, the person specification can and should be reviewed and revised regularly through discussion involving all the parties who may be concerned and, ideally, as part of a regular development process.

The person specification derives, in the first instance, almost entirely from the job description which dictates many of the skills and qualifications which will be required. The job description will certainly determine the minimum qualifications and will also give an indication of basic experience required. Table 8.6 illustrates in the right-hand column some headings for a flexible framework for writing a person specification for the whole range of positions in secondary schools. For the post of deputy headteacher the basic qualifica-tions are specified. The length and precise nature of previous experience is also evident from this person specification. The emphasis is again on clarity, evidence and precision. It is possible to be even more specific if we so desire. Is experience of a particular type of school or in a particular subject area desirable or essential? Are there particular aspects of the post which may demand experience in working with special equipment or with particular groups of children? Are the records of pupils to be transferred to the new computer and, if so, will the deputy require special expertise or be required to acquire it, especially as he has responsibility for liaising with feeder primary schools? Does the deputy head have the financial and administrative skills necessary to manage the school's budget? Has the deputy head sufficient experience of staff development and in-service training to provide support for colleagues in this area? These and many similar considerations help to shape a person specification similar to that which appears in Table 8.6. This table also shows how the job description and the person specifica-tion may be used in conjunction with one another to give a complete picture of one set of tasks within the school.

Some parts of the person specification, such as the qualifications, may pertain to the actual incumbent when the person profile was written, but these will need to be subject to revision if the present postholder leaves.

Parts of the specification may also indicate where it might be desirable for the postholder to gain additional qualifications or experience. If the specification came to be used as a basis for an interview then care would have to be taken to rewrite it with the future needs of the school in mind and to avoid the possibility of precluding the appointment of an excellent candidate who does not quite fit the preconceived ideas of the interviewers. Yet it should be sufficiently explicit to avoid the possibility of employing a square peg for a round hole.

To understand one's own function within the team as well as within the whole school and to have a similar insight into the work of professional colleagues can only assist in the smooth running of the school. For this reason alone, the process of completing school profiles, individual profiles and school development plans is beneficial. For similar reasons job descriptions and, ideally, their associated specifications should be known not only to the headteacher or team leader and the holder of the post, but shared with colleagues. Such sharing of knowledge can lead to a clearer and more supportive appreciation of what everyone in the school is doing and is trying to do. It can also help to establish the necessary unity of vision or common approach which is so helpful in achieving the aims of any school and in ensuring that those aims do not become divorced from reality. School profiles and job descriptions inevitably raise questions about what teachers are trying to do. This, in turn, helps everybody to develop a more informed understanding of the aims of the school and the ways in which it is hoped that they might be achieved. As a result, expectations become more realistic since they are based on knowledge rather than on speculation. Constraints are identified and understood, and the criteria for the adoption of particular forms of organisation are open to inspection and debate.

Taken as a whole the process of producing school and individual profiles, and the writing of job descriptions and specifications can make a valuable contribution to several major areas of school management and can have benefits for all staff of the school. Staff development and school development can play a vital part in ensuring that the most appropriate education is provided for the pupils in each school while, at the same time, helping teachers to maximise their own professional skills. A sound and objective base for staff deployment can also be identified from the analysis of the work of the school. Appraisal can take place on the basis of a clear understanding by all of what the school is trying to do, how it is trying to do it and what part each individual is playing in that process. Job descriptions, therefore, provide an essential framework within which appraisal can take place.

Activities

1 What techniques would you employ when constructing a profile to ensure precision and conciseness?

2 If you were writing an individual curriculum profile for one of your teachers what steps would you take to ensure that it was accurate?

3 Using the model in Table 8.6 construct a job description for your own post. Now construct the related person specification. Whom are you going to consult to see if these are accurate? When and how will you use them?

Chapter 9

Staff appraisal and the secondary school team

In the previous chapter we saw how important it was to have a clear job description and a related person specification. Job descriptions need to be re-examined and renegotiated from time to time. Similarly colleagues need the opportunity to talk through their work and professional development with team leaders or other senior staff. One method of achieving this is staff appraisal. A well-thought-out job description is a useful starting point for staff appraisal.

STAFF APPRAISAL IN SCHOOLS

Staff appraisal can be approached in a number of different ways. In the mid-1980s six LEAs were invited to embark upon pilot projects for the introduction of appraisal into schools. The results of those pilot schemes were reported in the recommendations of the National Steering Group (NSG) (HMSO 1989). Those recommendations can be summarised as follows:

(a) Appraisal should be introduced within a national framework, comprising regulations and guidance in the form of a DES circular.
(b) Responsibility for implementing appraisal for all LEA-maintained schools including voluntary-aided schools should rest with LEAs.
(c) The aims of appraisal should be those set out in the 1986 ACAS report. They should be set out in the regulations.
(d) Appraisal should respect and promote equal opportunities.
(e) Regulations should require LEAs to implement appraisal for all staff on teachers' conditions of service, except licensed, probationary and articled teachers.
(f) The headteacher should decide who should appraise each teacher in a school. The circular should specify that the appraiser should normally be the line manager of the teacher.
(g) Headteachers should have two appraisers, both appointed by the chief education officer of the LEA. One of them must have relevant experience as a headteacher.

(h) The appraisal of both teachers and headteachers should be conducted on a two-year cycle, with each successive two-year period treated as one appraisal programme.

(i) Each appraisal programme should have the following components:

- an initial meeting between the appraiser(s) and the teacher or headteacher being appraised (the appraisee) to clarify the purposes and to identify areas of work on which the appraisal might concentrate;
- self-appraisal by the appraisee;
- classroom observation for teachers (on at least two occasions) and either classroom or task observation (observation of the headteacher at meetings) for headteachers;
- review of other relevant information, the work of pupils, information about duties outside the classroom;
- an appraisal interview, providing an opportunity for genuine dialogue between the appraisee and the appraiser;
- preparation of an appraisal statement recording the conclusions of the interview, including agreed targets for future action/professional development; and
- a follow-up meeting to review progress, to be held in the second year of the programme.

(j) Appraisal should be conducted against the background of sound professional criteria.

(k) When collecting information for appraisal, appraisers should follow the code of practice set out in appendix 4 to the report.

(l) Access to appraisal statements should be restricted to the appraiser, the appraisee, the headteacher of the school and the CEO or nominated officer. Separate records of targets for professional development and training should be kept and these should be made available to those planning development and training at school and LEA level.

The NSG estimated that the cost of implementing these recommendations would be about £40 million per year. The then Secretary of State for Education, John MacGregor, responded to this report by initiating further consultations and by making appraisal voluntary. In December 1990 Kenneth Clarke, the new Secretary of State for Education and Science, decided to make appraisal compulsory for all teachers in order to develop the professionalism of teachers and so improve the education of their pupils. He argued that appraisal would assist teachers to realise their potential, carry out their duties more effectively, and provide opportunities of support for the weaker teachers. It would also afford parents a further assurance of the quality of teaching which their children receive.

The Secretary of State accepted the recommendations of the NSG on the aims and broad components of appraisal. It would take place on a two-year cycle. Its main feature would be the observation by a senior colleague of the teacher's work in the classroom followed by a discussion of the appraisee's professional development. This would lead to the setting of targets for future action. The first cycle of appraisal would be completed within four years from September 1992 (DES 1991). The essential feature of the NSG's report that was not accepted by the minister was the costing of appraisal. Financial support of around £10 million would be made available for each of the first two years of the process with final decisions about future costing to be made at a later date.

Apart from the obvious resource implications contained in this statement, the Secretary of State made at least three further significant points. He identified the professional development of teachers as the main purpose of the appraisal process. He drew attention to the need to identify and support weak teachers. He indicated that appraisal has a part to play in making teachers accountable to parents for the education of children (DES 1991). Each of these points echoes the debate that has raged about the appraisal of teachers in recent years. It is this debate that has helped to make the introduction of staff appraisal into schools a potentially hazardous exercise. This debate has led teachers to attach a range of meanings to appraisal and to the justification for its introduction. These have been discussed extensively elsewhere (Bell 1988; Poster and Poster 1991), although it is worth pointing out here that one of the most damaging of the justifications was its proposed use to identify incompetent teachers. This was based on the view that the teaching force needed to be cleansed of teachers who were in some way incompetent and who were probably responsible for the ills of the education system. The most outstanding example of this position can be found in Sir Keith Joseph's speech at the North of England Education Conference in January 1984 in which he argued that it was vital for incompetent teachers in our schools to be identified and removed. He pressed this view further in 1985 by asking students to comment on the comparative quality of teachers during private meetings on several visits to schools over a two-year period. This belief in the existence of a substantial number of incompetent teachers has proved difficult to sustain. Nevertheless, it is still implicit in a number of statements on appraisal emanating from DES publications. It can be found embodied in *Better Schools* (DES 1985a), in *Quality in Schools: Evaluation and Appraisal* (DES 1985c) and, as we have seen, in the Secretary of State's recent pronouncements.

A similar set of justifications attached to appraisal and based on the view that there is a significant number of weak teachers who need to be removed from the system in order to restore public credibility in education has been developed by Midwinter (1985). He justifies his support for teacher appraisal by arguing that 'surrogate consumers', that is parents, should have more say in teacher appraisal. This would, he argues, allay their anxiety about 'bullies, mental now more than physical' and the 'no hopers and nincompoops' as well as the 'idlers' who now teach in schools and who were recruited during the late 1950s and early 1960s when, it is argued, standards of entry were dropped at a time of acute shortage. Midwinter places considerable faith in the power of parents to assess who the 'good' and 'bad' teachers are, and goes on to argue that 'the lore of the launderette is unerringly accurate'.

These two sets of justifications have in common the view that there is considerable room for improvement within the teaching profession. Their point of departure is over how such an improvement might best be brought about. The search for incompetent teachers as envisaged by the DES would be carried out according to the criteria set out in DES publications and would presumably use those staff appraisal procedures which the LEAs would establish. From Midwinter's perspective, appraisal would be carried out by groups of parents acting as vigilante representatives of all the parents for a particular school. Quite how this process would work was never spelled out.

Strangely enough, a similar perspective emerges when the views expressed by headteachers and LEA representatives are considered although, in this case, incompetence is replaced by demoralisation and the appraisal process would be carried out by teachers themselves within their own schools. The use of staff appraisal for motivational purposes is well documented in industrial circles. The extent to which this deliberate provision of a Hawthorn Effect will work is not clear but the assumption that it will is certainly built into a number of management courses and has also been made by HMI who argue that in many cases appraisal procedures

> lead to a better working climate and to improved performance by the school and by individual teachers.

> (DES 1985c: para. 141)

Perhaps the least threatening of the inherent sets of meanings as far as teachers are concerned is that which links staff appraisal to the professional development of teachers. This view was part of the rationale advanced by Kenneth Clarke in his statement about the introduction of compulsory staff appraisal in schools. It also emerged both in the documents produced by LEAs such as Northamptonshire and Croydon and also in DES publications. In *Teaching Quality* (DES 1983) it was argued that those managing the school teaching force have a clear responsibility to establish policy for staff development and training based on a systematic assessment of every teacher's performance. Staff appraisal schemes which are geared primarily to identifying in-service needs or other kinds of experience that might enhance career development appear to be, at least in part, acceptable to many teachers if the views expressed in the publications of teacher unions are to be accepted as a guide. This view of appraisal is certainly the one adopted throughout this chapter. The assumption is made here, therefore, that the rationale behind the introduction of any staff appraisal system into a secondary school is that its main intention is to provide opportunities for professional development for the teachers in that school.

In fact, the appraisal of teachers is not at all new since all promotions depend on some form of appraisal. What is new is the introduction of legislation to ensure that the performance of teachers is regularly appraised (DES 1991). No definition or description of the appraisal interview is given in this legislation. It might simply take the form of an individual teacher asking herself questions and, perhaps, discussing her answers with a colleague. The questions could be:

- What are the tangible results of your job being well done?
- What happens when your job is not well done?
- In order to improve your performance, on what should you spend more time/effort/imagination?
- How can you best be helped to improve your performance in these areas?
- What will the tangible results be of such an improvement in performance?

These questions are relatively non-threatening in themselves. They will help all teachers to fulfil what has been called the fundamental principle of staff appraisal: that of improving the education of pupils in schools. In spite of a recognition on the part of many teachers that 'all teachers need help in assessing their own professional performance and in building on their strengths and working on limitations identified' (DES 1985a: 13), the context within which much of the discussion of staff appraisal has taken place has helped to focus on the difficulties and disadvantages of staff appraisal rather than on its benefits.

The major difficulties associated with the introduction of staff appraisal tend to focus on the natural suspicion that many teachers have of such a change in their working conditions. This suspicion has manifested itself in a number of ways.

(a) Any form of staff appraisal is often regarded by teachers as a direct attack on their own professional autonomy. Teachers have, in the past, exercised this autonomy within their classrooms almost to the exclusion of all other forms of influence. A staff appraisal process which impinged on the right of teachers solely and entirely to make professional judgements about activities within the confines of the classroom would threaten that jealously guarded privilege.

(b) Suspicion is also expressed by some teachers about the ability of their colleagues in middle or senior management to carry out an effective appraisal process or to implement such a process impartially, because of past problems or past professional relationship difficulties. These two basic suspicions lead to a natural reluctance to accept this change.

(c) Teachers also feel that they would be placing themselves in a highly vulnerable position if a staff appraisal process required them to indicate those areas of their professional life where they were experiencing difficulties or were requiring help or further training. It is felt that such information might prejudice promotion prospects or lead to a general diminution of their esteem within their school.

(d) It is also argued that staff appraisal, if carried out badly, would increase the level of cynicism within the schools and lead to a lowering of teacher morale.

Apart from these concerns, a major barrier to implementing staff appraisal effectively is believed to be the extent to which those training needs or staff development needs identified by the process could or would be met by the school or the LEA. Clearly, in order to overcome the suspicions and concerns any staff appraisal process needs to be introduced into a school carefully and effectively. This will mean that all of those to be involved in such a process will require training before the system can be introduced. The extent to which such training is required and the time that it would take is also identified as a difficulty when introducing an appraisal system. Concern is expressed about the extent to which LEAs and schools could provide the necessary training and the extent to which those people who are to be in the position of appraisers would recognise that such training was necessary.

None of these difficulties associated with staff appraisal can be resolved easily. It is incumbent on those who wish to introduce such a system into schools to take account of these difficulties and to seek to overcome them in a variety of different ways. There is no doubt, however, that the major disadvantage of introducing staff appraisal into schools is the fact that it will consume a significant amount of scarce resources, both in terms of time and money. It is unrealistic to expect an appraisal process to be carried out outside normal working hours. Therefore, the resources have to be provided in order to free those people who are involved in the process so that they can meet, prepare for and conduct appraisal interviews and also so that they can follow up the interviews effectively. Resources will also be required in order to meet the training needs which such a process undoubtedly will identify on the assumption that the introduction of a systematic appraisal system into all schools will require:

- central administration;
- release time for all teachers;
- training for headteachers, deputies and heads of departments;
- secretarial costs.

Apart from the cost in resource terms the other major disadvantage associated with the introduction of staff appraisal is the cost in personal terms. An effective process requires honesty and courage in the application of the process to all colleagues. It requires objectivity and the ability to separate personal relationships from professional relationships. It also requires those involved to recognise that appraisal can provoke conflict and controversy, but that it need not do so if staff are well trained and are committed to carrying out the process effectively.

In order to see how this might be done we need to consider the question, 'What is staff appraisal?' in the context of managing teams in secondary schools. Simply stated, appraisal is an opportunity for both the appraisee and the appraiser to stand back and take stock of performance over the past two years, to examine how far targets which were agreed at the last appraisal have been realised, and to identify new targets. Appraisal is not an opportunity to criticise any individual's personality or opinions, or to discuss other colleagues. It should focus specifically on the individual teacher's own performance within the school. It provides an opportunity to explore with that teacher:

* how well she is performing;
* whether she can improve in any areas;
* actions to improve her performance;
* ambitions and aspirations;
* potential for taking on more demanding jobs;
* actions to develop new skills;
* views and feelings about the job and the school or department.

CLASSROOM OBSERVATION AND TEACHER APPRAISAL

If the above areas are to be explored then observing the teacher at work in the classroom must become a necessary part of the appraisal process. Such observation will, however, only be one aspect of the total process of gathering information on which to base an appraisal interview. Any method of observing teachers working with their pupils will need to be valid and reliable, to avoid subjectivity and bias, and to take account of the difference between performance and competence. These matters are best grasped by team-based discussions to draw up a set of criteria for classroom observation that is appropriate for the work of that team.

Such discussions must lead to an observation procedure that is valid in the sense that it correctly picks out teachers who are successful and differentiates them from those who are less successful. The procedure must also be able to identify the extent to which appropriate learning outcomes are achieved by the pupils since teaching is essentially a means to an end, that of pupil learning. The procedure must be reliable in that it can enable accurate differentiations to be made over a period of time in the variety of different contexts within which members of the team may find themselves. It must also minimise the possibility of observer bias and subjectivity determining the results.

When drawing up a procedure for classroom observation the team must make a distinction between measuring performance and identifying competence. A teacher's competence is made up of the skills, abilities, knowledge and beliefs that are relevant to the process of teaching and that the teacher brings to the classroom. Together, these tend to be relatively consistent and stable over time. Teacher performance is the behaviour of the teacher in the classroom as she plans, teaches and evaluates her work. This is the product of the environment in which she works, including pupil behaviour, team management, school organisation, personal and social factors. Teachers may, therefore, be far more effective with one class than with another or perform better at some times than others.

Teaching and learning are integral parts of the same process. It follows, therefore, that any team seeking to establish a procedure for classroom observation is well advised to consider what it regards as good classroom practice and to make that explicit as a starting point for its discussion. The team might conclude that pupils learn best when work in the classroom:

- is well planned with clear aims and objectives which are shared with and understood by the pupils;
- starts with the needs of the pupils, whether individually, in groups or as a class;
- uses a variety of approaches and methods;
- harnesses pupils' natural curiosity by means of starting points which challenge, motivate and reward;
- makes regular and thoughtful use of first-hand experience;
- encourages the use of the imagination;
- draws on the pupils' environment for starting points;
- seeks to help all pupils to fulfil their potential, especially those whose performance may be influenced by factors outside the school's control such as a pupil's sex or social, cultural or linguistic background;
- creates opportunities for pupils to achieve, whatever their particular strengths and abilities;
- allows pupils to lead and support, to offer and respond to ideas, to offer and accept suggestions and criticisms, and to take and share responsibility;
- uses language which is clear, precise and economical and which modifies or expands explanations to suit pupils' needs;
- emphasises skills, the processes by which pupils learn, as well as content, so that pupils develop to plan, to evaluate, to research and to apply skills;
- for pupils with marked learning difficulties breaks activities down into a series of small achievable steps;
- offers easy access to necessary resources;
- engages pupils actively in their learning;
- encourages pupils to experiment with a variety of responses;

- allows pupils enough time to produce work of quality and depth;
- allows/encourages pupils to exercise choice;
- encourages pupils to take responsibility for their own learning;
- builds on the knowledge, concepts and skills developed in previous years;
- ensures that pupils receive feedback on their progress – feedback which as far as possible is positive, thereby helping to foster a positive self-image;
- records carefully pupils' strengths and weaknesses as a means of planning their next tasks.

When addressing the matter of classroom observation in the context of teacher appraisal most of the pilot projects adopted a clinical supervision approach. This has three essential features:

- a preparatory discussion to clarify the purpose of the observation, to establish the objectives of the observation, the nature of the class being observed, the aim and objectives of the lesson, and to agree on the time, place and nature of the feedback;
- the observation itself conducted on the basis of agreed criteria and in an agreed way;
- the feedback session in which teacher and observer share information, decide on the nature of future observations and agree actions to be taken. This then informs the main appraisal interview;

This approach may require a sequence of observations rather than a single one. It is time consuming, but it ensures that classroom observation is developmental rather than judgemental. It must be based on agreed criteria and recorded in an agreed way. Some teams may wish to list a number of factors that might be considered. These might include:

- planning and preparation of the lesson;
- beginnings, endings and transitions between activities in the lesson;
- selection and presentation of material;
- appropriateness of content and activities;
- communication including verbal and non-verbal skills;
- recognition and catering for individual differences;
- discipline and control;
- use of equipment;
- assessment of pupils' work;
- record-keeping and use of records to plan.

Other teams might wish to pose a series of questions about the teaching that is being observed. Such a list might include:

(a) *Understanding of objectives:* How well does the teacher understand (and describe) the objectives of the lessons or work undertaken? How sound is her understanding of the subject matter?

(b) *Preparation:* Are the lessons or work prepared thoroughly and to the point? When visual aids are required, are they chosen effectively?

(c) *Teaching Skills:* Is the lesson content balanced and varied within individual lessons and between lessons?

How effectively has this been kept?

How skilful is the teacher in using the spoken and written word to communicate with pupils?

How well does the teacher use extra information or ideas arising during the lesson?

How perceptive is the teacher to the needs of individual pupils? How adaptable in catering for their different abilities and rates of progress? Is adequate guidance given?

How well is pupils' interest maintained and developed?

How competently are the lessons or work introduced and concluded? How well does the teacher deal with transitions between different phases of the lesson? When materials are used are they cleared away satisfactorily?

How appropriate and relevant is the range of activities expected from pupils? How effectively are pupils advised and guided?

How able is the teacher at using questioning techniques and at encouraging discussion?

(d) *Pupils' work/assessment:* How appropriate, given age and ability, is the quality of the pupils' work? Is it ever displayed or otherwise used for the benefit of others? How satisfactorily marked or assessed are the various activities of the pupils? How efficiently has the teacher recorded each pupil's progress? Has this led to any adaptation in teaching methods and work set?

(e) *Evaluation:* How well does the teacher assess relative strengths and weaknesses and use lesson evaluation to plan future work?

A similar approach might be based on a series of statements describing the ideal state which team members wish to achieve in their teaching. The observer in this case would comment on how far each intention had been met. Such a series of statements might include:

(a) *Clarity of aims:* The purposes of the lesson are clear.

(b) *Appropriateness of objectives:* The aims are neither too easy nor too difficult for the pupils. They are appropriate and are accepted by the pupils.

(c) *Organisation of the lesson:* The individual parts of the lesson are clearly related to each other in an appropriate way. The total organisation facilitates what is to be learned.

(d) *Selection of materials:* The content is appropriate for the aims of the lesson, the level of the class and the teaching method.

(e) *Selection of materials:* The specific instructional materials and human resources used are clearly related to the content of the lesson and complement the selected method of instruction.

(f) *Beginning the lesson:* Pupils come quickly to attention. They direct themselves to the tasks to be accomplished.

(g) *Clarity of presentation:* The content of the lesson is presented so that it is understandable to the pupils. Different points of view and specific illustrations are used when appropriate.

(h) *Pacing of the lesson:* The movement from one part of the lesson to the next is governed by the pupils' achievement. The teacher stays with the class and adjusts the tempo accordingly.

(i) *Pupil participation and attention:* The class is attentive. When appropriate the pupils actively participate in the lesson.

(j) *Ending the lesson:* The lesson is ended when the pupils have achieved the aims of instruction. There is a deliberate attempt to tie together the planned and chance events of the lesson and relate them to the immediate and long-range aims of instruction.

(k) *Teacher–pupil rapport:* The personal relationships between pupils and the teacher are harmonious.

(l) *Variety of evaluative procedures:* The teacher devises and uses an adequate variety of procedures, both formal and informal, to evaluate progress in all of the aims of instruction.

(m) *Uses of evaluation to improve teaching and learning:* The results of evaluation are carefully reviewed by teacher and pupils for the purpose of improving teaching and learning.

This list is, in fact, a series of performance indicators that can help teachers to organise their work in classrooms. Yet another possible approach is for the observation to be based on some measurement of performance either on a scale of 1 to 5 or according to an agreed range, (see Table 9.1 for an example). Each variation has its advantages and disadvantages. The one based on measurement gives a feeling of objectivity and may enable comparisons to be made over time. Its weakness lies in the possible interpretations of the scale. One observer's average may be another's good, while, even for the same observer, good may be different on different days. The other approaches have similar weaknesses although each of them seeks to define in different ways what each criterion means. The most important factor in establishing a procedure for classroom observation is that agreement is reached between those observing and those being observed about what the relevant criteria are and how they are to be interpreted. All parties need to understand the procedure once it is adopted. They also need to know how the data collected will be used and how it will inform the appraisal interview.

Table 9.1 A checklist for observing a teacher's classroom performance

	1	2	3	4	5
	Very poor	*Weak*	*Satisfactory*	*Good*	*Very good*
Purpose/intended outcome					
Preparation of materials					
Relevant pupil activities					
Individual differences					
Initial motivation					
Communication					
Questioning					
Class control					
Guiding/advising					
Conclusion of lesson					
Marking/assessing					
Recording					
Evaluation					

THE APPRAISAL INTERVIEW

Appraisal is a sensitive issue so that its introduction has to be carried out with diplomacy and with the full co-operation of the staff. It is important from the outset to involve all members of staff in the discussion about the proposed process and to respond openly to their natural fears and reservations. Many teachers approach the idea of performance evaluation with some anxiety, Nevertheless, as Table 9.2 shows, there can be significant benefits for both the individual and the school from appraisal. There is a better chance of getting these benefits as a result of appraisal, rather than through daily contact, because the appraisal interview is a chance to stand back from day-to-day work pressures.

Appraisal needs to have a standard structure for everyone who is being appraised. It is important to treat everyone in the same way. Questions might be arranged in the following sequence:

- What are the most important areas of the teacher's role?
- What are her strengths – what has she done well?
- What are the main problems she has encountered?
- Can these problems be avoided in future?

Table 9.2 The benefits of staff appraisal in schools

Benefits for the individual	Benefits for the team leader, headteacher and the school
Knowledge of where she stands regarding the rating of her performance.	A better understanding of how staff are satisfied with their work.
Knowledge of where she is going in terms of improvement and development plans.	The opportunity to plan for improvements in performance.
Obtaining help to improve and develop.	The opportunity to plan the best use of ability and potential.
Gaining a greater sense of belonging through realising the value of her contribution to the school.	An insight into the effectiveness of the management of the school.

- What are her staff training and development needs?
- What is the best way to achieve each improvement?

The above points deal with teacher performance in their present post. They should be approached through a discussion of a job description such as that described in the previous chapter. If an interview is to cover future opportunities as well, the following areas can be explored:

- What abilities, if any, are not being fully used in her present post?
- What new tasks could she take on in the coming year?
- Does she want to take on more demanding jobs?
- What is the best way to develop each new skill?

Finally, if it is intended to check job satisfaction during the interview, the following points could be included:

- What aspects of the job give her most satisfaction?
- What caused any dissatisfaction?

Guidelines to enable both the appraiser and the appraisee to prepare for the interview have to be prepared (see Table 9.3). All those involved need to be briefed about them. Six questions can be used as a basis for the interview. Both the appraisee and the appraiser should respond to them in writing in readiness for the appraisal interview.

(a) *Performance.* Consider your performance and comment on your most important achievements. Itemise particular results and successes with which you were involved. (In subsequent interviews this question

Table 9.3 Preparation for staff appraisal

Make arrangements
- Set a date, time and place for the appraisal interview.
- Allow at least 60 minutes for the interview.
- Give at least two weeks' notice of the interview to the member of staff, to allow her time to prepare.
- Brief her on how to prepare, running through the interview outline.

Appraiser's preparation	*Appraisee's preparation*
Before the interview go through each interview question, noting important points, using all relevant information including that from classroom observations.	Before the interview, go through each interview question to decide responses.
Concentrate on training and development needs, and ways to satisfy these needs.	Concentrate on: – things that have gone well; – problems; – training and development; – aims for the next year.
Provisionally decide realistic training and/or development aims for the next year.	Think of realistic training and/or development aims for the next year.
Consider whether any problems might arise during the interview and plan how to handle them.	Think of ways to achieve improvement aims with guidance or support.

would refer to the period of time since the last appraisal interview). Have there been changes to your job that might need to be reflected in a modified job description?

(b) *Disappointments:* Consider your present performance and comment on any disappointments with respect to your own responsibilities.

(c) *Obstacles:* What factors outside your control hindered you from achieving a better performance?

(d) *Training and new experiences last year.* What training or new planned experiences did you undergo last year? In what ways have they helped?

(e) *Increased skill or knowledge.* What part of your present job could benefit if you received additional training or new planned experiences?

(f) *List of training needs:* As a result of completing the whole form, list the areas of training or planned experiences you need in order to further develop your professional expertise.

There is an advantage to both parties if the appraiser has a copy of the answers to these questions in advance of the interview. She is then able to:

- read carefully through the appraisee's responses and decide the areas of agreement and omission;
- concentrate on what has gone well and improvement needs;
- think of realistic improvement or development targets for the future;
- think about ways in which she could help or support the member of staff to achieve her targets.

Each interview must be planned in detail, basing the approach on two principles. First, the appraiser asks the appraisee to comment on each issue and then the appraiser comments on that response, adding additional points where necessary. Second, the appraiser moves from the appraisee's strengths to any weakness that may exist, finishing on a set of agreed actions to improve the situation and to foster the professional development of the colleague. These agreed actions are to be written down and a copy provided for the appraiser and the appraisee showing clearly what has been agreed, what has to be done, by whom, by when and, where relevant, to what standard or criteria. If this approach to appraisal is followed then the process will be seen by all team members as supportive and developmental. It will emphasise performance within the context of agreed targets and identified ways of enhancing the professional development of the appraisee. In this way staff appraisal can make a significant contribution to staff development within the team and throughout the whole school.

Asking a member of staff to prepare is an important stage in appraisal. It helps to gain commitment, so that both parties treat the appraisal as a genuine opportunity for improvement. In the new climate for staff appraisal, where classroom observation takes a central place in teacher appraisal, it is important that team members see the process as supportive and developmental. An emphasis on performance within the context of agreed targets will help to achieve this. A well conducted appraisal interview in which the team leader appraises the work of her colleagues based on an existing job description, will enhance the professional performance of team members and provide them with an opportunity to reflect on, and further improve their professional practice. Good preparation by both the appraiser and the appraisee, and sound organisation are the keys to effective staff appraisal in schools. Such an approach to appraisal will make a significant contribution to staff development within the team and throughout the whole school.

ACTIVITIES

1 Devise and apply a schedule for classroom observation based on the examples given in this chapter.
2 Identify the steps you would need to take in order to implement staff appraisal in your school.

3 Prepare your own answers to the six questions suggested on pages
  137–8. Discuss them with a colleague. What personal professional
  development needs can you identify?

Chapter 10

Conclusion: Development, change and stability

Teacher appraisal, as outlined in the previous chapter, highlights the extent to which the management of staff has become an important part of the secondary school team leader's role. Added to this is the need for team leaders to be able to cope with the more general and increasingly demanding tasks of managing change and creating a stable environment within which all members of the team can work. In all of this, however, staff development has a vital part.

STAFF DEVELOPMENT

The team leader has three crucial roles in staff development.:

- as the exemplar of good practice, appropriate attitudes, acceptable behaviour and commitment to her pupils and staff;
- as initiator of many of the individual programmes of staff development and in-service training;
- as the facilitator who makes staff development happen for team members.

School development planning will help the team leader to do all of this more effectively. This will, in turn, require that team members and team leader embark upon a dialogue about school, team and staff development needs. Such discussions must be carried out within the framework of what the school is trying to achieve. Thus, team development has to be linked to both individual and school development needs in such a way as to ensure that the maximum individual professional development can take place while still ensuring that the aims and objectives of the school can be achieved.

Staff appraisal and whole school development should emphasise the formative and developmental aspects of both processes. One possible approach, based on a detailed discussion by the whole staff of the aims and objectives of the school, its various needs and the development requirements of the staff, is illustrated in Figure 10.1. Here full consideration of the needs of the school takes place in parallel with the introduction of staff appraisal so that discussions in one area can inform those in another. The

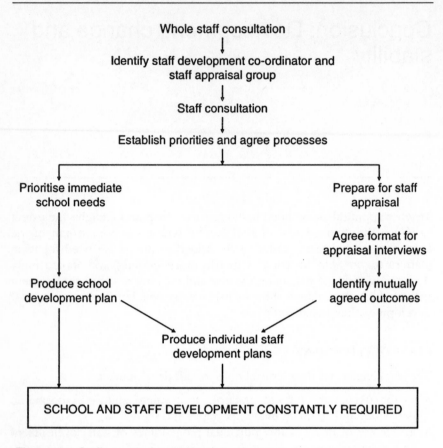

Whole staff consultation

Identify staff development co-ordinator and
staff appraisal group

Staff consultation

Establish priorities and agree processes

Prioritise immediate
school needs

Prepare for staff
appraisal

Agree format for
appraisal interviews

Produce school
development plan

Identify mutually
agreed outcomes

Produce individual staff
development plans

SCHOOL AND STAFF DEVELOPMENT CONSTANTLY REQUIRED

Figure 10.1 Staff appraisal and school development

process outlined in this figure might begin with a whole staff consultation
out of which a group responsible for managing the process would be
identified. Most schools, to meet the obligation to manage in-service education placed on them by LMS, already have a staff development co-ordinator
who should be involved in the process. If a supporting group of colleagues
can be identified, the ownership of the process can be more widely shared.
As a result of discussion at school, department, year or other functional
group level, the main priorities for the school might be identified and agreed
upon before appraisal interviews start. In this way the action plans which
will result from the appraisal interviews can be informed by the discussions
on the school's immediate needs. The professional development of
individual teachers can, in this way, be more closely linked to the priorities
of the school. In turn this will make it more likely that those needs can and
will be met. The meeting of individual staff development needs is perhaps
the single most important factor in ensuring its success and the production

of the desired outcomes for pupils: that is an improvement in the quality of the education which they receive. This may well be achieved, at least in part, through a staff development programme which is a planned sequence of experiences designed to enhance the knowledge and expertise of teachers.

Producing a staff development programme for a school, therefore, needs to be based on a clear understanding of what it is that the school is trying to achieve, as well as on a knowledge of the professional development needs of its teachers. Such a programme may also take into account two further sets of factors. First, specific steps to remedy situations in which the work of the school does not always proceed quite as smoothly as might be wished, especially where such situations are a result of a lack of knowledge, skill or expertise on the part of the staff; and second, the changes which are likely to affect the school over the next few years.

Wherever possible such factors should be part of the information used to identify a staff development programme because they help to ensure that the school is as well prepared as it can be to respond to changes in a positive fashion rather than having to react to them hastily.

Once the content of the staff development programme has been identified it has to be implemented. Table 10.1 illustrates the potential richness of professional development opportunities that can be made available to many teachers, often at little or no cost. If the two main options still remain either to hold in-service sessions in school or to go elsewhere for INSET, what should influence the decision?

There is evidence to suggest that choices about professional development programmes are taken in a relatively arbitrary way, often without reference to the long-term needs of the school and of individuals within the school (Cowan and Wright 1990). The in-service days which are the major part of current professional development strategies of many schools and LEAs have undoubtedly enhanced the ability of teachers to make choices and to meet their own needs. One recent investigation concluded that in-service days provided by and for specific schools:

- encouraged better staff co-operation;
- encouraged better use of facilities;
- have led to improved strategies for all school systems, discipline and resources;
- helped to establish school appraisal scheme;
- provided time to exchange ideas;
- created opportunities to visit, liaise with colleagues in other departments and institutions;
- helped schools develop policies;
- raised staff awareness;
- helped to highlight specific needs.

(Derived from Cowan and Wright 1990: 117)

Table 10.1 Some further strategies for staff development in schools

Activity	Application
Project work	To match individual (or group) development needs with a project such as developing new teaching material. Useful if you want your colleague to stand back from day-to-day activities, or if you are seeking to encourage initiative.
Information collection	To establish a basis of hard fact. Also useful for developing organising and fact-finding skills, and attention to detail.
Information analysis	To develop skills in interpretation, evaluation and decision-making.
Planning	To contribute to or take responsibility for the planning of all or part of a team's programme. Helps to develop the practice of thinking before acting.
Problem-solving	To use problem-solving techniques. Helps to develop objectivity, reasoning and decision-making skills.
Written report preparation	To improve written communications, and ability to think logically and reason things out.
Oral report presentation	To make formal presentations to you at stages in the plan (reporting back), or to a group. A particularly good activity for developing the skill of communication with other people.
Observing someone else	To study an alternative approach to task performance – possibly assessing the performance against a check-list of key requirements. A useful step in delegating, or in trying to overcome a weakness, by providing a model of required performance.
Standing in for you	To obtain experience in management or another task, through temporary delegation.
Undertaking a different role	To do part of someone else's job, on a temporary basis. Useful for broadening experience, or to realise effect of own performance shortfalls on others.
Planned visiting	To find out more about other schools or about industry or commerce. Useful for gaining better insights into alternative ways of doing things provided key observational points are agreed in advance.
Self-study	To report back on a particular issue after a period of directed study of relevant books or other materials with a specific brief.

At the same time, however, the same training days:

- failed to match the needs of the school as a whole;
- did not ensure that individual needs were met;
- were not usually evaluated by staff to ensure both an avoidance of mistakes next time and continuing commitment from staff to any plans or policies formulated;
- occurred at times which were inappropriate or unhelpful for immediate follow-up;
- were not based on long-term professional development plans;
- had themes which often occurred in isolation and without regard for previous or subsequent activities.

(Derived from Cowan and Wright 1990)

Equally, day or longer courses provided as part of a staff development programme from outside the school may:

- be too theoretical;
- reflect priorities determined by providers;
- not reflect school needs;
- not have practical application in the classroom;
- ignore teacher expertise;
- be expensive;
- require long-term commitment.

Table 10.2 shows how a choice between school-based and externally provided staff development can be made so that the chosen programme is most beneficial for the school and for the staff concerned. The message is clear. Do not use a course just because it is there, but do not base everything on the school simply so that financial resources can be eked out. Make the choice on the basis of what is possible at any given time.

If after careful consideration it is decided that the most effective form of staff development is to use an externally provided course, then the implementation of this process ought to be carried out as thoughtfully as would be the planning of a school-based programme. The following guidelines can help to ensure that this is done. Before the course:

- check that the course objectives meet the needs of the proposed participant.
- give her as much notice as possible.
- be sure she knows where the course is and what she has to take with her.
- discuss what you expect her to gain from the course: check your staff development plan and the training results you are seeking to achieve.
- where possible inform the course organiser what you want your colleague to achieve.

Table 10.2 Choosing a strategy for implementing staff development

For each part of the staff development programme there are two options

School-based INSET	*Away from school*
One of the staff or a consultant will provide in-service training.	Provision by the LEA or other provider.
Choose school-based INSET:	*Choose away from school training*
When a member of staff has the skills and time required to give instruction or a suitable consultant is available.	When there is a course which is appropriate in timing, in achieving the results required and for the level of person requiring training.
When it is the most cost-effective way.	When such a course will be cost-effective.
	When attitude changes are required which are best achieved by mixing with others in similar posts.
When the skill and method are specific to the school or department and no courses are available.	When staff have neither the skills nor the time to give the instruction.
	When the resources exist to meet the costs and to provide cover for the colleague on the course.

After the course:

- discuss the course, arrangements, people attending and the quality of presentation.
- identify what your colleague felt she gained from the course.
- agree actions that will be taken as a result of the course, when and how the effect can be measured.
- remember to check that the agreed actions are taken, and the results achieved. Give further help yourself if necessary.

Within the school team there is often a range of other options available for implementing staff development. At the very simplest level these might include briefing a colleague in a planned and formal way on a new task; coaching a colleague on the performance of a new task; and embarking on a programme of development for an individual or group over a period of time when the skills or tasks to be understood are complex and require practice. If the team leader undertakes staff development at any of these levels she should ensure that she discusses the following points with the colleague involved:

(a) *The reason:* Explain why you have selected your colleague for the particular training and why you are planning it at this time

(b) *The task:* Explain and agree precisely what you require and the targets or standards of performance.

(c) *Control:* Discuss your availability to confer on any problems, how you will be kept informed about progress and whether there is a need to delegate some of her duties after training.

(d) *Attitude:* Check that she is keen to take on the training and that she has enough confidence to tackle it.

The team leader should ensure that all other members of staff who are likely to be affected know about this part of the staff development programme.

There is a range of related activities which can be incorporated into different kinds of staff development programmes to suit individual colleagues or to meet the needs of all or part of the staff group. Some of them have been touched upon elsewhere in this book but all require careful preparation based on a clear and explicit understanding of what is to be achieved by the exercise. Targets need to be set at each stage. Table 10.1 provided a summary of some useful activities and an indication of when they might be used.

For each type of strategy adopted to implement part of a staff development programme, whether it is for the whole school, a group or an individual, the basic principles to be followed are the same:

* Plan the programme thoroughly in advance on the basis of what is to be achieved.
* Carry out an initial briefing with those involved in that part of the programme and ensure that outcomes, expectations and targets are understood.
* Monitor progress while the programme is being implemented and make any necessary modifications.
* Follow up the programme by taking the necessary steps to ensure that the agreed actions are carried out since this is the only way that the school can benefit from the in-service training of its teachers.

Planning a staff development programme requires detailed preparation whether it is for an individual, a group of colleagues or the whole staff. The following points in the example which follows refer to an individual colleague but they are also useful for planning whole school in-service days:

(a) *Define results:* It will help you and your colleague if you identify what you want her to do and decide on performance standards.

(b) *Decide methods:* How can necessary skills and attitudes be developed to achieve the result? Stages may include watching or helping you, doing jobs under your supervision or attending training sessions.

(c) *Agree programme:* Gain agreement and commitment on the stages in the programme, the timing of each stage and resources required, and the dates when progress will be reviewed by all those involved.
(d) *Use programme:* While the development is going on check progress at each stage, offer help, advice and encouragement if needed and modify the programme to cope with delays or difficulties.

One final step remains. That is to review the planning, implementation and follow-up to ensure that it was as effective as possible and that future parts of the programme are well planned and carried out. This review should focus on the questions listed in Table 10.3. These can be asked of all forms of staff development activity whether for individuals or groups of teachers. The essential features remain the same.

Much of the above discussion on staff development, staff appraisal and school evaluation has sought to show that all staff have a role to play in each of these processes although these roles may vary according to the position or responsibilities held. These functions, like the more general management of the school, are not the sole responsibility of the team leader but of the whole staff team, each of whom will make a contribution according to qualifications, expertise and experience. Such contributions will also be determined by the opportunities offered or created by and for her. Team leaders have a vital role to play in this regard for they are often in a position to initiate and develop such opportunities. However skilful a team leader may be in doing this, such activities require, at the very least, the tacit approval of the headteacher. The extent to which this is true of any individual headteacher will depend on her view of her own role within the school, her assessment of the school and its requirements, her skills and abilities and, perhaps above all at this present time, her perceptions of the internal and external changes which face schools at the end of the twentieth century. However this is viewed, the management of change is, and will remain, an essential part of the management of all secondary schools and the teams within them.

MANAGING CHANGE

George Bernard Shaw once remarked: 'Reformers have the idea that change can be achieved by brute sanity.' Yet change cannot be successfully introduced simply by defining a desired state and letting other people achieve it by following your plan. The introduction of any change will involve stress, anxiety and conflict. It will be muddled and may require carefully formulated plans to be modified or even abandoned. Change, therefore, is a complex and messy process, not least because it is a process of intensive interaction even within the smallest staff team.

This interaction forms part of the context of the change. People react to change and its challenges in different ways. This cannot be managed by

Table 10.3 Reviewing staff development strategies

Staff development	*Colleague development*
PLANNING	
Was the target clearly defined and realistic? If not, what further actions are required?	Has the target been achieved?
Was your choice of activities sufficiently imaginative?	Can your colleague now perform the task or fulfil the new role without further staff development? Or will further actions be needed?
Did the sequence of actions and timing prove sound?	
Did you gain your colleague's involvement and commitment?	
CARRYING OUT	
Did you check progress frequently enough?	How has your colleague reacted to the staff development experience? Is there a favourable attitude to further coaching in other tasks?
Did you let your colleague know how well she was progressing?	
Were you successful in overcoming problems?	What is your colleague's next development need? Should you start on it immediately or hold off for a while?
STAFF DEVELOPMENT SESSIONS	
Did you prepare sufficiently?	How have the rest of the staff responded to this process?
Did you work to clear aims?	
Did you involve your colleagues fully?	
Was your manner encouraging?	

intuition alone for, as Heller (1985) reminds us, some people will support the change while others will oppose it. Some supporters of change may be evolutionary in their approach. They are prepared to spend much time building firm foundations on which the change may rest. Others may be much less patient and more aggressive in their approach. Of those who oppose the change some may actively fight against it while others may passively or truculently resist it. These attitudes become part of the context within which change takes place. Any change, however much it is needed and welcomed by most of those involved, will meet with resistance.

Where the change affects the work of the team it is the responsibility of the team leader to attempt to manage the change in such a way as to minimise the resistance, the conflict and the hostility that will be generated. The extent to which the change is resisted will, to some extent, depend on what the change is. A move from one mathematics scheme to another produces resistance which is different from that encountered with the introduction of new forms of teamwork, for example. On the other hand, resistance can be increased by the nature of the situation and by the use of poor change techniques by team leaders. Where the reasons for the change are not made clear or are presented in such a way as to be unacceptable to those people most likely to be affected by the change, resistance is more likely to be encountered. Team members must be able to participate fully in exploring the need for change before any decision about the nature and the extent of the proposed change is taken.

Agreeing on the need for change is the first stage in minimising conflict and resistance. This has to be done independently of the management of the specific change. The second stage is having a specific set of objectives for the change which are fully understood by those involved and ensuring that these are communicated in a form in which they can be used to monitor and evaluate the change.

In this way all team members can check for themselves on the progress and direction of the change. All the members of the staff team involved in any type of change are likely to be concerned about the way in which it is going to affect them. They may worry about how a structural change will influence their promotion prospects or about whether they have the necessary skills to cope with it. These concerns are often made worse by a lack of understanding about the present and future situations, and by a feeling on the part of the individual team member that she has no ownership of the change which is taking place and therefore cannot exert any influence over it. Resistance can also be brought about by pressure of work since, when people feel overstretched, having to cope with the introduction of change is the last thing that they will want. Where team leaders do not take into account the existing work patterns and the ways in which pressure in any team will fluctuate, they can increase the problems caused by pressure of work during the change. This makes the process more difficult than it might otherwise be. Such problems emerge when those responsible for the change fail to consider how that change might best be planned.

PLANNING AND CHANGE

The decision to plan any change can be seen as an attempt to impose direction and purpose on anticipated future events. As was seen in chapter 6, planning usually requires the identification of objectives to be achieved in the medium or long term rather than an attempt to match a set of immediate and unco-ordinated responses to a perceived situation. Embodied in these objectives may be an attempt to improve an undesirable situation. Planning also requires that the various members of the team integrate their efforts to meet the overall objectives. This frequently leads to a situation in which people working in different parts of an institution need to learn more about its total function and about their role and that of others. Previously held assumptions and modes of operation may need to be questioned and even changed if the objectives are to be achieved.

It has been said that if you do not know where you are going, any road will get you there, although it might well be asked how you will know that you have arrived. From the point of view of any school, planning is deciding where to go, how to get there and how to know when you have arrived. Planning is a continuous activity by which an organisation changes and is thus different from a plan which is merely a set of decisions for action in the future. The continuous nature of this process is frequently overlooked.

Planning is also preparatory to action. Analytically at least, planning must be separated from implementation so that the major policy decisions can be taken and their implications understood prior to action. Unfortunately this can lead to a situation in which vital revisions are not made because the planning process, mistakenly, is thought not only to be preparatory to action, but also to conclude once implementation commences. As a result, the required resources may not be mobilised at the appropriate times to ensure successful implementation. This can often lead to agreement about ends but disagreement about means. Interlocking, interdependent and often sequential sets of decisions need to be made in order to reproduce an activity which is broader than decision-making. The action which stems from these sets of decisions is central to the process since planning is directed towards achieving action in certain areas rather than, say, acquiring pure knowledge.

With careful planning, then, resistance to change can be, if not eliminated, at least minimised by involvement, by communication, by awareness and by the nature of the process itself. Involving all the people who are going to be affected by the change provides them with a basis for understanding what is going on and an opportunity for them to influence the change which, in turn, can generate ownership of it and commitment to it. Involvement also enables team members to have access to information about the change. Once people are informed then rumour and misunderstanding can be confronted and overcome. Sharing information allows discussion to take place. This, in turn, creates an awareness of what the problems, opportunities and intentions are. A team which is characterised by such openness in its relationships and by a supportive environment in which problems and differences can be shared, is likely to be able to cope with the difficult process of changing. Resistance to change will be lowered when people know why a change is being introduced and what advantages are likely to result from it.

For the leader of the secondary school staff team, managing change effectively means that she has to be able to predict what the likely outcomes of the change are; prepare for the change as team leader and so prepare others; identify potential problem areas and the action required to deal with them; implement the change itself; and recognise and exploit the opportunities which the process of change may produce. These abilities must be seen in the light of two most basic questions.

- Is the change really needed?
- Are the likely outcomes worth all the effort and upheaval which the change will produce?

If the answer to both of these questions is positive then the change must be managed. This can best be done by following a seven-stage process.

Analysis

The first stage in the management of the change process is that of analysis. Change will always be easier to manage if, within the team, there is general agreement on aims, division of responsibilities, fair distribution of work, effective arrangements for delegation and a reasonably efficient communication system. The importance of these factors has been discussed in previous chapters but, before embarking on any planned change, time spent by the team leader in reviewing them is time well spent. The team should be clear about the demands which are currently being placed upon it, or which are likely to emerge in the immediate future. It can then have a more realistic view about the feasibility of the planned change. Team leaders therefore need to analyse the change in terms of where the team is now in relation to where it wants to be in the future, and also in terms of what factors are helping and what are hindering the team in its efforts to achieve the desired change.

A force field map can help with this. It also helps in understanding why a change is being resisted, since the very process of active listening will begin to reduce resistance to the change. This type of analysis was first devised by Lewin (1947). It is based on the premise that a change situation is a balance between two sets of forces. The process has nine developmental steps which are:

Step one: Identify clearly the problem or issue. Identify and describe the change including methods to be used to sensitise others to it. Note that the description is required in writing so that a record is available.

Step two: Define the change in terms of the current situation including staff attitudes to change and the desired situation including a definition of an acceptable state.

Step three: List driving and restraining forces. Figure 10.2 shows how this is done diagrammatically. The thicker the arrow, the more powerful the force. The longer the arrow, the more long-lasting the force. These forces include anything that can hinder or help the change: technology, material, methods, people, time and money. What is important is to be specific.

Step four: Highlight those forces considered to be most important.

Step five: List actions which might reduce or eliminate the restraining forces highlighted.

Step six: List actions which might increase the driving forces which have been highlighted.

Step seven: Determine the most promising measures which could now be taken and identify the available resources.

Step eight: Re-examine the actions and place them in sequence, omitting any that do not seem to fit.

Step nine: Implement and evaluate.

The management of change must therefore be firmly based on an approach which has defined what the change is to be, has planned how to bring it about and has identified ways of coping with the difficulties which must arise during the process of change.

Having done this it is now possible to think about the future. What is the desired future state towards which the planned change is moving the team? What will be the consequences of doing nothing? The answer to that question is, at this stage, the most crucial of all because it determines just how necessary it is to change anything at the present time. The whole of the team should be involved in and take responsibility for this analysis since such involvement is vital in order to get the commitment necessary from the team members to enable the change to be managed successfully.

Diagnosis

After the analysis comes the diagnosis of the problem. Even where a proposed change is clearly the result of a perceived problem, team leaders should ensure that the problem is fully understood by all members of the team. The team as a whole must agree that the proposed change will, in fact, provide the necessary solution to the problem as identified. It is easy for problems and solutions to become loosely attached to each other. The solution proposed, while it may be acceptable to many people on educational, philosophical or even practical grounds, may not actually provide a solution to the real problem. For example, giving colleagues more time in which to write record cards will not be a solution if the problem is that the cards are too complex or require information which teachers are not easily

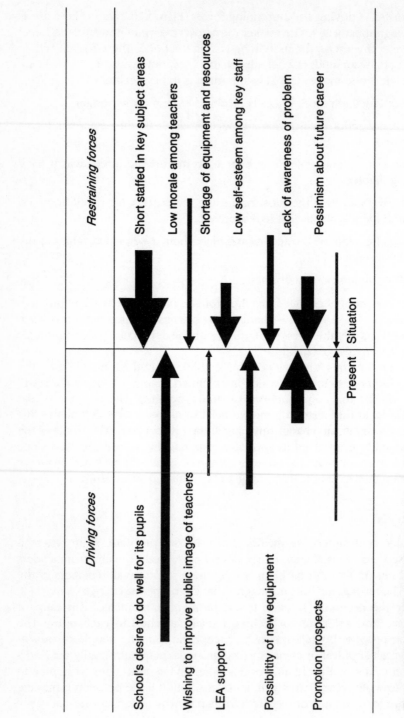

Figure 10.2 A force field model – present situation

able to provide. Whatever the initial diagnosis of the problem, the team leader should seek to confirm it from a variety of sources before embarking on any action. This is not a licence for inactivity: if the initial diagnosis is wrong then everything which follows from it will be wrong. It is wise to collect as much data as possible about the situation by talking to team members and others with relevant knowledge and information, by observation and by looking at all the quantitative data that exist in the school.

This step is perhaps the simplest and yet the most important. It is relatively easy to recognise that there is a problem of some kind, but recognition does not identify what the problem is, and certainly does not suggest any solutions. It is necessary, therefore, to seek answers to questions such as:

- What is wrong?
- Where within the school organisation is the problem located?
- Who or what is affected?
- When is the problem evident?

Some ways of collecting information are listed in Table 10.4. Accuracy and, as far as possible, objectivity are essential at this stage. Incorrect identification of the problem may cause severe difficulties at a later stage. An initial identification of a problem should only be accepted after it has been confirmed from a range of sources.

Examining alternatives

On the basis of a thorough analysis of the present situation and careful diagnosis of the potential problem it is now possible to begin to identify solutions. The team leader has to ensure that all alternative possibilities are considered. The first solution which is offered should not be accepted simply because it is the first or apparently the most likely, or because there is considerable initial support for it. Team leaders should, at the very least, ensure that as many ideas as possible are considered in the early stages of examining alternatives. This, contrary to how it might at first appear, is time well spent.

A simple technique such as brainstorming can be used to generate, from within a team in a very short time, a large number of possible alternative courses of action. A well-run brainstorm session will produce ideas that may range from the totally wild and silly to the brilliant and perceptive. It is essential that no idea is rejected: even those ideas which appear to be extreme. These serve several functions. They generate laughter which, in itself, is an excellent catalyst and prevents uneasy silences which are the very death to effective brainstorming. They also encourage those team members who might otherwise be reticent to put forward ideas. A brainstorm is easy to arrange if a few simple rules are followed. The initial preparation has to

Table 10.4 Ways of collecting information

Interviews	A straightforward but subjective way of obtaining information, but one which will usually serve as a good starting point from which to gather more detailed information. For effective interviewing: • decide what information is wanted and from whom; • interview a representative sample of the people involved; • ask a few key questions; • encourage open-ended responses.
Observations	Structured observation can clarify issues related to a particular problem area. It should: • be carried out by more than one person looking at the same thing; • be recorded together with any evidence; • be reviewed by the observers collectively.
Option surveys	Often helpful in establishing opinions about priorities and performance held by different people in school. They have the merit that they can: • cope with a fairly large population and also be quantified and compared; • be used as a basis for small group discussions between people involved in the problem area.
Quantitative information	An often neglected area of information for those involved in the management of change in schools. It can: • compare individuals or groups; • illustrate changes over time; • be visually displayed (for example, histograms or graphs).
Group discussion	Small group discussions between people most involved with the problem area create opportunities for real involvement. Discussions: • can focus on differences of opinion; • give everybody an opportunity to comment on the nature of the problem and suggest possible solutions to it; • may attempt to place possible causes and suggested solutions in rank order; • can link to the next stage in the process, looking for alternative solutions.

be carried out and shared with the team. This means that the present situation and the nature of the problem have to be analysed as described previously. The problem has to be stated to the team at the start of the brainstorm and accepted so that the session concentrates on generating solutions, not debating the nature of the problem. Team members need to have had time to think around the problem before the session but, by involving them in the process of analysis, the team leader will already have ensured that this has happened.

When all this has been done and the team is ready, the brainstorming session itself can begin. A member of the team should record and display all the ideas as they are raised in such a way that they can be easily seen by the whole group. This role does not prevent the leader or recorder from joining in. The team is asked to give as many solutions as possible to the stated problem. While this is going on, while the ideas are being shouted out, it is essential that all judgement is suspended. Clarification must also be reserved until the exercise is complete.

The brainstorm finishes when no more ideas are forthcoming. The session, itself, is not yet over. The team leader now asks the team to evaluate the ideas. Each team member is asked to examine the list and without discussion to select between 10 and 20 per cent which she thinks are worthy of further consideration. The leader collects the lists and identifies which ideas have the most support. These can then be considered in more detail.

Decide upon the preferred solution

From the previous stage a series of possible alternative solutions emerge. Each of these should be subjected to detailed discussion by the team in the light of the analysis and definition of the problem. From this, a preferred solution can be identified. This should be subjected to further discussion. A series of questions might be asked about the chosen solution. In what ways can this idea go wrong? Who needs to be involved in or consulted about this? What skills and knowledge does the team need in order to implement the change? Are they available? A more limited brainstorming technique can be applied to generate answers which can be taken into account at a later stage.

Plans can now be prepared to implement the change, bearing in mind that the planning will be developmental and innovative. These plans should state clearly what the objectives are and how they are to be achieved. They are translated into a series of priorities which are in turn translated into direct action by named individuals. The objectives are simply those changes which have to be made within the school in order to solve the problem or to improve the situation. They should state what has to be done, by whom and in what sequence. These actions become the key tasks which combine to make up the action programme for implementation. The programme should also indicate to what standard an activity or task must be done and what resources are necessary. All the actions in the programme should relate to the diagnosis of the problem.

At this stage, it is often useful to set out the programme in the form of an action grid as in Table 10.5, or a series of action grids. The actions here should be stated in positive terms, the outcomes of which can be identified. To plan, to list, to design, to read, to convene and to identify can all be seen to have practical outcomes; to understand, to consider, to know or to appreciate do not. Resources should be clearly stated together with any additional help which will be required. All of the tasks in the action programme can be summarised in this way.

Managing the transition

The planning of the change process should be formulated in such a way as to include those steps which are necessary in order to move from the present state to the desired future state. The plans should also recognise that there is an intermediate stage between the present and the future: the transition state. Leaders and their teams should appreciate that transition from one stage to another takes time. It cannot be achieved immediately. Change takes time. As time passes tasks associated with the management of the change have to be accomplished. While this is going on, the day-to-day running of the school and the part played in it by the team have to continue. Routine does not cease in order that change can be brought about; ideal though this state of affairs might be. The transition has to be managed.

The secret of successful transition management is to create a structure staffed by people whose main responsibility is to ensure that the change is successful and takes place as smoothly as possible. They should not necessarily be those people who will be responsible for running the changed situation. Transition management structures are temporary and should be disbanded when the change is complete. The team leader may wish to choose a small group from within the team to do this. Such a group might include the natural leaders in the team or those with special and relevant skills. The team leader should be associated with this group, but not necessarily be part of it since the rest of the work of the team has to continue and this will require much of the team leader's attention. The transition management group will have the special responsibility of making those organisational arrangements which are necessary for bringing about the change. This has to start with a plan. Planning may be handled by the transition management team alone. However, it is more likely that the team leader will be fully involved and that the rest of the team will participate in the progress, for it is at this fifth stage that rumours begin to fly, anxieties to develop and misunderstandings occur. Effective communication is vital and a wide understanding of what is afoot is important.

Table 10.5 Action grid

Task	Person responsible	Resources required	Outcome	Deadline	Performance level	Further action
To collect a number of examples of maths schemes suitable for secondary children.	Head of mathematics department.	Current catalogues. Secretarial assistance for ordering. Display in maths teaching area.	Completed delivery from publishers by spring half-term.	Planning meeting: 14 November.	At least four schemes, including all three recommended in county maths guide.	All members of planning team to have seen copies before planning meeting. Item on staff meeting 18 Nov: to introduce staffroom display. 18–30 Nov: staffroom display. 1–2 Dec: feedback meetings.

Implementation

The group responsible for managing the transition will have the main role to play in the implementation stage. This will be based on the agreed plan. This plan should be adaptable so that it can cope with those unforeseen problems which will arise and those tasks which will not, in spite of everyone's best endeavours, be completed on time. It should be cost-effective in terms of time and people. It must be remembered that everyone involved within a team in the management of change, including the transition management group, will have normal teaching duties to fulfil and that the change is imposing additional work. It may be enriching or rewarding. It may be regarded by the team leader or her colleagues as a vital and necessary part of staff development, but it still means that plans have to be realistic.

Once the plans are formulated the change process can move to the sixth stage: that of implementation. It must be remembered that no change can be implemented successfully unless it has the commitment of, or at least is acceptable to all those likely to be affected by it. Commitment and acceptance are integral parts of the same set of attitudes. Acceptance implies an agreement to the implementation of change; commitment implies a willingness to play a positive role in bringing about the change. The most effective way of gaining acceptance and commitment is to ensure that there is general agreement about the nature and importance of the problem together with an understanding of how the proposed change will solve it.

It may be necessary for the team leader or the transition management group to cope with a number of barriers to change. These are often expressed as 'I can't see that working here', or 'We have tried all that before'. Such statements are often an indication of hurt and anxiety which have to be talked through and dealt with as part of the process of managing the change. They should neither be ignored nor be allowed to assume more importance than they deserve. By involving colleagues from the outset, such problems can be seen early and can be minimised.

Successful implementation depends on ensuring that the benefits of the change are recognised by those who are doing the work. Where team members are spending their time and energy on a project, they should see the benefit from the results of their efforts. This means that they need to be told about what is going on, about how well the plans are working, as well as where the problems are. The team leader has to ensure that team members have the training and support necessary to implement the change. The implementation stage requires as much time and effort as the preceding stages but, by this time, team members are often running out of energy or having their attention diverted elsewhere by other tasks. The team leader must ensure that the implementation is followed through according to the plan, and where necessary reminding those who have accepted responsibilities of their obligations.

It is helpful if one member of the group, possibly the person who is monitoring progress, ensures that communication is effective at this stage. Are those who have to give approval for actions being consulted? Are those who should be informed of actions being involved? Are the appropriate and promised resources forthcoming? Above all, perhaps, are the changes which are taking place still moving the team in the direction in which it originally wished to go, and is this still the right direction? This, above all else, must be constantly monitored especially in the later stages when some of the changes already made may create situations which were not foreseen in the original plan. Each of the different tasks in the programme must therefore be expressed in terms which contain an element of evaluation such as a deadline and a statement about levels of performance. Throughout the implementation stage, the person or group with overall responsibility for managing the change should make periodic checks on the effectiveness of what is being done.

Monitoring and evaluating

Monitoring the tasks involved in the change process is necessary to ensure that implementation is taking place in the way in which it was designed or to enable implementation procedures to be changed as the need arises. It prevents the pattern which occurs all too frequently of evaluating a response to a problem only after a task is completed or a change fully implemented. Monitoring during the implementation stage increases the likelihood that difficulties can be identified and corrected. It also serves as a useful reminder that flexibility at this stage is of crucial importance. Such flexibility must be based on the evidence produced by monitoring in the light of the objectives agreed in the earlier stages.

Monitoring should be given high priority, since many promising innovations have come to grief because staff have shifted their attention to other matters once it appears that the solution to a particular problem is in sight. Continual monitoring will prevent this from happening. Monitoring has to be done on the basis of the original agreed definition of the problem, the identification of the preferred solution, the plan of action which was designed in order to bring about this desired future state and the implementation of that plan. Monitoring and evaluation can be used as a trigger to help sustain energy and motivation for the change as well as to examine the progress of all or part of the change process. For mature evaluation during the change attention should be focused on the relationship between the priorities, the direction of the change and the intended desired state. The team leader, above all others, has to be sure that the change is taking the team in the desired direction and that the priorities remain the same after the process of change has begun. Everyone involved in the change process should be kept informed about the results of monitoring and evaluation especially where this leads to some modification of the original plans for action. By keeping people informed and involved, the team leader can minimise anxiety and therefore reduce the possibility that resistance to the change will develop as the change progresses.

The summative evaluation of the results of the change after the process is completed may need to take place over an extended period of time. This, of course, will depend on the nature of the change and the intention behind it. The criteria for evaluating the change need to be derived explicitly from the stated objectives for the change as established at the start of the change process or as modified while the change was being implemented. A simple set of questions asked of colleagues might also help. Such questions might include: Are the pupils learning more effectively? Did we move far enough in the agreed direction? Did the priorities remain the same? Answers to these questions will give an indication of the extent to which the problem was solved. More information may be required. The collection of further information should be preceded by establishing what it is that should be known, why it needs to be known, and how it will be used.

There is a limit to the amount of time, resources and staff effort that can be expended on any problem. Summative evaluation may have two key elements. The first will be to look at the success of the change with reference to, for example, items in the following list derived from Pountney (1985):

- Formal testing through end-of-year examinations, standardised tests, quizzes or short written tests.
- Pupil profiles written by themselves and teachers.
- Observation of pupils in the classroom and around the school.
- Progress records kept by the teacher.
- Comparisons with other schools and national or local statistics.
- Advice from other colleagues, outside agencies, parents and others in the community.
- General impressions of classrooms, displays, teacher–pupil relationships and pupils' attitudes.

The second will consist of an attempt to establish whether or not further expenditure of resources on a particular problem is worth the effort. This is a realistic rather than a cynical approach to evaluation since it recognises that schools have to operate with limited or reducing resources in the light of which it is often necessary to ask: Have we done the best we can with this problem, and is it time to concentrate on something else?

Leaders of secondary school teams are, almost inevitably, going to be faced with situations in which they are required to bring about changes or where their teams are going to be involved in changes within the school. Managing change is difficult because change itself generates tension, conflict and anxiety. Team leaders should adopt a planned approach to change based on the assumption that to cope with the process of managing change effectively and efficiently it should be an activity which is shared by all those who are likely to be affected by it. If team leaders are prepared with their teams to devote time and effort to the management of change, then it can be done successfully.

MANAGING STABILITY

Throughout this book it has been argued that the staff team has a collective responsibility for management and that individual teachers have specific responsibility for particular aspects of the work of the school. It has been argued that teams can be managed more effectively if all staff are involved in the process of management. It has been suggested that, in some circumstances, in responding to change for example, most of the staff must participate if the enterprise is to succeed. The essence of these processes is, as Tomlinson has suggested, that the secondary school staff team should ensure that:

- aims and objectives are clarified;
- methods for teaching and learning are chosen and applied;
- evaluations and assessments of the results are made.
- what is learnt from the judgements is fed back to improve the aims and the methods.

(Tomlinson 1987: 9)

These processes should be continuous and natural. They should involve the whole staff as well as parents, governors and others who co-operate with the teachers. Thus, the assumption which underpins the management processes which have been explored in the preceding chapters is that authority and responsibility within the team should be shared. Indeed it has been suggested in the early chapters that if the school is to be managed effectively, and for the maximisation of staff expertise to ensure the optimum long-term benefit for all the pupils, then such sharing is a necessity. For this to happen a certain stability has to be achieved.

One of the major factors in establishing and maintaining stability in any staff team is the extent to which the team has confidence in the leader. Torrington and Weightman (1989b) remind us that a team leader can achieve this by her approach to team management. Colleagues will have confidence in a leader who:

- has a fair but firm management style;
- leads by example;
- is open and provides support and reassurance;
- shares work and resources equitably;
- is consistent in her dealings with colleagues;
- encourages everyone to work as a team;

- respects the views of others;
- stands up for the interests of the team and its members.

The effective team manager will also adopt a thoroughly professional approach to the work of her team based on:

- knowledge of each member's subject or field of interest;
- belief in the value of the work of the team;
- being a good practitioner in areas of the work of the team;
- valuing the expertise of others within the team.

The approach to management implied here is the one which has been advocated throughout this book. The point about valuing team members is especially important at a time when over one in three teachers in secondary schools are actively considering leaving the profession. The most significant reason given for this is that teachers are misjudged and seriously undervalued.

> Teachers tend to feel a lack of consideration from their colleagues when the . . . [team] culture is one of keeping to oneself rather than talking to colleagues.
>
> (Torrington and Weightman 1989b: 31)

Teachers can be made to feel valued in a number of ways; some of which have already been explored in depth in previous chapters. For example, colleagues feel valued when an important task with real responsibility is delegated to them. This shows that they are trusted and that the team leader has confidence in them. People also feel valued when they are informed about, consulted on and involved in decision-making. This, together with good communication, helps to create a feeling of belonging to a team. Similarly a fair and effective appraisal process can help colleagues to feel valued by giving them feedback on their performance and identifying ways of supporting them in the future. If colleagues within the team experience a feeling of being valued then they are more likely to make a worthwhile contribution to the work of the team. They are also less likely to opt out or to want to leave for other than sound professional reasons. A team which values its members will tend to be a stable team.

Team stability can also be enhanced by a greater awareness on the part of both the team leader and the team members. The individual team member should always be aware of the part that she has to play in the team. Each team member should know:

- her duties within the team and the extent and limits of her roles and responsibilities;
- how she contributes to the overall work of the team;
- the standard of performance that she is expected to achieve;
- how satisfied the team leader is with her current performance;

- her prospects for promotion and increased responsibility;
- plans for the future development of the team;
- her contribution to those developments;
- the ways in which her work has an impact on that of her colleagues;
- her responsibilities to others in the team.

A similar set of points might also be made about the contribution that the individual teacher makes to the work of the school as a whole. The individual team member will feel a greater sense of belonging to the team as a result of the awareness that comes from having the knowledge outlined above. This can only help to make the team a happier and more stable unit in which to work.

In addition to the management skills that have been explored in the previous chapters, a team leader's awareness has to be based on her knowledge of individual team members. For each team member the team leader should know:

- how far she is aware of the points listed above;
- what motivates her most;
- how satisfied she is with her job;
- her future career aspirations and ambitions;
- her professional development needs over the next few years;
- how well she gets on with the other team members;
- any problems she has in carrying out her work;
- any problems she has that affect her work;
- how easy she finds it to discuss her work with the team leader.

At the same time the team leader, in conjunction with the headteacher and the senior management of the school, may need to explore further ways of maintaining a stable team. This may, in the future, focus on the need to keep and develop existing staff. How effective, therefore, is the school's staff development policy? Is it working? Is there a school policy on job sharing? Is there a policy on job rotation within the school? How can these policies best be applied to the team? How are part-time staff incorporated into the life of the school and how does the team support its own part-time members?

If teams are to remain stable and function effectively they must be adequately resourced. Team leaders cannot increase the level of resources going into their schools although they may be able to influence the allocation of those resources within the school, especially now that schools receive delegated budgets. Gaining an increase in resource allocation at the expense of other teams within the school may not always be desirable. Nevertheless team leaders do need to know how resources are allocated within their schools if they are to exert any influence on that process.

It is incumbent on team leaders to understand and be able to operate within the processes of resource allocation used in their schools. Team leaders will also need to adopt a fair and sensible strategy for allocating resources within the team. One way of doing this is:

- to allocate a percentage on a loose historical basis within the team, although monitored by a formula to detect any significant changes in need and usage;
- to retain a percentage for general costs;
- to reserve a relatively small amount for special situations, new or one-off developments;
- to put in place a method of monitoring and controlling the team's expenditure on a monthly and termly basis by keeping a running total of projected spending matched against actual expenditure.

Such a system is relatively simple and fairly quick to operate. It is able to respond to changes in circumstances and to make some allowance for special developments and it has built-in checks to help control expenditure. It can be made even more effective if team leaders have a sound plan for expenditure over two, three or more years based on an accurate assessment of historical and current costs. For example, team leaders should know for their team:

- current and projected expenditure on books and materials;
- current and projected expenditure on reprographics;
- current levels of stock;
- the rate at which books, equipment and materials are used up or lost;
- the rate at which relevant books and equipment wear out and will need to be replaced over the next three years.

On the basis of such knowledge resources can be more efficiently managed within the team. Team members will feel that each is being treated fairly and that the best use is being made of the available resources to support the work of the team.

Team leaders can also contribute to the stability of their team by representing it within the school at large. This could be termed marketing the team and its work. A distinction has to be made here between the external marketing of the school in the community at large and the representation of the work of the team in the internal market of the school community. Team leaders will not normally have an external marketing function but they will have an internal role to play. The internal market will normally consist of colleagues including support staff, pupils, parents, governors and voluntary helpers.

The team will need to establish which groups, at any given time, are the important ones to reach when marketing a particular aspect of its work. This will obviously depend on circumstances. It might be that the team is seeking to gain support for a project requiring substantial additional resources. The marketing target group would be those whose support was necessary to influence the decision.

As well as establishing who is to be reached, the team must identify what is being marketed and why it is being marketed. Such an analysis can be based on the strengths, weaknesses, opportunities and threats (SWOT) approach. Methods of promoting the idea or project will have to be identified and implemented. These might include discussion groups, meetings, memos, brochures, posters, displays of work or presentations by teachers and/or pupils. Once the marketing strategy has succeeded then quality has to be controlled and monitored. Approaches to monitoring and evaluation have been discussed in detail in previous chapters. These processes are essential to the successful marketing of the team and its work within the school.

Marketing like every other aspect of team management in secondary schools must rest on a clear recognition of the strengths of the team; on an acknowledgement of where the team must improve its performance and of how this is to be done; on giving the team a sense of purpose and direction within the overall context of the school; and on achieving a measure of stability for the team, yet not allowing it to stagnate or rest upon its laurels. These are the challenges that face all members of every team in every school.

This concluding chapter has argued that effective team management in secondary schools depends upon the ability of team leaders to develop their staff, to cope with change and to establish and maintain a degree of stability within the team. Team leaders have an important part to play in establishing and maintaining stability within their teams. This can be achieved by finding ways to value team members and by having a coherent set of strategies for delegating to them and involving them in the work of the team. Team leaders and members must be aware of their roles and responsibilities within the team. Consideration must be given to alternative staffing arrangements and to appropriate forms of resource management. The team must be represented and marketed effectively within the school to ensure that its strengths are recognised and built upon. An effectively managed team will, therefore, be one in which these processes are carried out on the basis of shared responsibility. Team members must be valued for the contribution that they make to the team and given appropriate support as well as opportunities for further professional development. Team leaders have to ensure that this happens within their teams.

ACTIVITIES

1 Establish the immediate staff development needs of your team. How would you construct a programme over the next year to meet all or some of those needs?

2 Identify one change that you expect your team to have to make in the next year. Draw up an action plan for implementing that change based on a force field analysis. State what has to be done, when, by whom and to what standard. What resources will you need to implement this plan?

3 List all the ways in which members of your team can be made to feel valued.

4 Draw up a plan for enhancing the status of your team within the school. Who will be your target group? What will be the unique features of the work of your team that you wish to emphasise? How will you set about implementing your plan? How will you judge its success?

Bibliography

ACAS (1986) *Agreement on Teachers' Pay and Conditions of Service*, Coventry.

Adair, J. (1983) *Effective Leadership. A Staff Development Manual*, Gower, Aldershot.

Adams, N. (1989), *Times Educational Supplement*, 17 February.

Beckett, C., Bell, L. and Rhodes, C. (1991) *Working with Governors in Schools*, Open University Press, Milton Keynes.

Belbin, R.M. (1981) *Management Teams. Why They Succeed or Fail*, Heinemann, London.

Bell, L.A. (1985) *Teacher Attitudes to Appraisal: A Survey of Conference Members*, University of Warwick, Department of Education mimeo., Coventry.

Bell, L.A. (1986) *The Organisation of Primary Schools: A Survey of Headteacher Perceptions*, Education Department, University of Warwick, Coventry.

Bell, L.A. (1987) 'Appraisal and schools', *Management in Education*, vol. 1, no.1, pp.30–4

Bell, L.A. (1988) *The Appraisal of Staff in Schools: A Practical Guide*, Routledge, London.

Bell, L.A. (1989) *Management Skills in Primary Schools*, Routledge, London.

Bell, L.A. and Arnold, F. (1987) 'Introducing staff appraisal to schools', *School Organisation*, vol.7, no.2, pp.193–208

Bell, L.A. and Day, C.W. (eds) (1991) *Managing the Professional Development of Teachers*, Open University Press, Milton Keynes.

Bell, L.A. and Maher, P. (1986) *Leading a Pastoral Team*, Basil Blackwell, Oxford.

Best, R., Ribbins, P. and Jarvis, C. (eds) (1980) *Perspectives on Pastoral Care*, Heinemann, London.

Blanchard, T., Lovell, B. and Ville, N. (1989) *Managing Finance in Schools*, Cassell Educational, London.

Bollington, R., Hopkins, D. and West, M. (1990) *An Introduction to Teacher Appraisal*, Cassell, London.

Broadfoot, P. (1979) *Assessment, School and Society*, Methuen, London.

Bush, T., Glatter, R., Goodey, J. and Riches, C. (eds) (1980) *Approaches to School Management*, Harper & Row, London.

Campbell, R.J. (1985) *Developing the Primary Curriculum*, Holt, Rinehart & Winston, Eastbourne.

City of Birmingham Education Department (1990) *School Development Plan. A Strategy for Management (Draft Document)*, City Council, Birmingham.

Coopers & Lybrand (1988) *Local Management of Schools; A Report to the DES*, HMSO, London.

Coulson, A.A. (1977) 'The role of the primary head', in R. Peters, (ed.) *The Role of the Head*, Routledge & Kegan Paul, London, pp.92–108

Cowan, B. and Wright, N. (1990) 'Two million days lost', *Education*, 2 February.

Davies, B. and Ellison, L. (1990) 'School finance. The management development plan', *Management in Education*, vol.4, no.4, Winter.

Davies, B., Ellison, L., Osborne, O. and West-Burnham, J. (1990) *Education Management for the 1990s*, Longman, London.

Day, C., Johnstone, D. and Whitaker, P. (1985) *Managing Primary Schools: A Staff Development Approach*, Harper & Row, London.

Dean, J. (1985) *Managing the Secondary School*, Croom Helm, London.

Dennison, W.B. (1989) *The Management of Resources. Module 4, Local Education Authorities Project Management in Education*, BBC, Milton Keynes.

DES (1972) *Teacher Education and Training (The James Report)*, HMSO, London.

DES (1977a) *Education in Schools: A Consultative Document*, HMSO, London.

DES (1977b) *Ten Good Schools*, HMSO, London.

DES (1979a) *Aspects of Secondary Education in England. A Survey by HM Inspectors of Schools*, HMSO, London.

DES (1979b) *A Framework for the School Curriculum*, HMSO, London.

DES (1981) *The School Curriculum*, HMSO, London.

DES (1982) *Mathematics Counts: Report of the Committee of Inquiry into the Teaching of Mathematics in Schools (The Cockcroft Report)*, HMSO, London.

DES (1983) *Teaching Quality*, HMSO, London.

DES (1985a) *Better Schools*, HMSO, London.

DES (1985b) *Education Observed 3: Good Teachers*, HMSO, London.

DES (1985c) *Quality in Schools: Evaluation and Appraisal*, HMSO, London.

DES (1985d) *The Curriculum from 5 to 16: Curriculum Matters 2*, HMSO, London.

DES (1985e) *Better Schools*, HMSO, London.

DES (1986a) *The Education Act*, HMSO, London.

DES (1986b) *Report by Her Majesty's Inspectors on the Effects of Local Authority Expenditure Policies on Educational Provision in England 1985*, HMSO, London.

DES (1987a) *The Education (School Teachers' Pay and Conditions) Order*, HMSO, London.

DES (1987b) *Financial Delegation to Schools: A Consultation Paper*, HMSO, London.

DES (1987c) Report by HMI.

DES (1988a) *The Education Reform Act*, HMSO, London.

DES (1988b) *The Management of Educational Resources, Effective Secondary Schools*, HMSO, London.

DES (1988c) *Secondary Schools: An Appraisal by HMI*, HMSO, London.

DES (1989) Regulation 14/89.

DES (1989a) *School Teacher Appraisal: A National Framework, Report of the National Steering Group on the School Teacher Appraisal Pilot Project Study*, HMSO, London.

DES (1989b) *1988 Secondary School Staffing Survey – First Results*, HMSO, London.

DES (1989c) *The Education (School Curriculum and Related Information) Regulations 1989*, HMSO, London.

DES (1990) *Press Release 389/90, Teacher Appraisal to be Compulsory*, DES, London.

DES (1991) *The Education (School Teacher Appraisal) Regulations 1991*, HMSO, London.

DES Welsh Office (1987) *The National Curriculum 5–16: A Consultation Document*, HMSO, London.

Dockrell, B., Nisbet, J., Nuttall, D., Stones, E. and Wilcot, B. (1986) *Appraising Appraisal*, British Educational Research Association, Birmingham.

Drucker, P. (1968) *The Practice of Management*, Pan, London.

Earley, P. and Fletcher-Campbell, F. (1989) *Time to Manage: Department and Faculty Heads at Work*, NFER-Nelson, Windsor.

Easen, P. (1985) *Making School Based INSET Work*, Open University Press, Milton Keynes.

Elliot, G. (1981) *Self-Evaluation and the Teacher*, Schools Council (mimeo), London.

Elliot-Kemp, J. (1981) *Staff Development in Schools. A Framework for Diagnosis for Industrial Teacher Development Needs*, Pavic Publications, Sheffield.

Everard, K.B. and Morris, G. (1985) *Effective School Management*, Harper & Row, London.

Fayol, H. (1916) *Administration Industrielle et Generalle*, Translated by C. Storris (1949) as *General and Industrial Management*, Pitmans, London.

Field, D. (1985) 'Headship in the secondary school', in Hughes *et al. Managing Education*, pp.308–24.

Goodworth, C.T. (1979) *Effective Interviewing for Employment Selection*, Business Books, London.

Georgiades, N.J. and Phillimore, L. (1975) 'The myth of the hero innovator and alternative strategies for organisational change', in C.C. Keirnan and F.P. Woodford, (eds) *Behaviour Modification with the Severely Retarded*, Excerpta Medica, Elsevier, North Holland.

Hall, V., Mackay, H. and Morgan, C. (1986) *Headteachers at Work*, Open University Press, Milton Keynes.

Handy, C. (1984) *Taken for Granted: Looking at Schools as Organisations*, Longmans, London.

Hargreaves, D., Hopkins, D., Leask, M., Connolly, J. and Robinson, P. (1989) *Planning for School Development: Advice to Governors, Headteachers and Teachers*, HMSO London.

Harling, P. (ed.) (1984) *New Directions in Educational Leadership*, Falmer Press, Lewes.

Havelock, R.G. (1970) *The Change Agent's Guide to Innovation in Education*, CRUK, University of Michigan, Ann Arbor.

Heller, H. (1985) *Helping Schools Change. A Handbook for Leaders in Education*, Centre for the Study of Comprehensive Education, York.

HMSO (1989) *Recommendations of the National Steering Group on School Teacher Appraisal*, London.

Hoyle, E. (1974) 'Professionality, professionalism and control', *London Education Review*, vol.3, no.2, pp.15–17.

Hoyle, E. (1981) *Managerial Processes in Schools: Part 1 The Process of Management, Block 3, E.325*, Open University Press, Milton Keynes.

Hoyle, E. (1986) *The Politics of School Management*, Hodder & Stoughton, London.

Hughes, M., Ribbins, P. and Thomas, H. (eds) (1985) *Managing Education. The System and the Institution*, Holt, Rinehart & Winston, Eastbourne.

Hume, C. (1990) *Effective Staff Selection in Schools*, Longman, Harlow.

Humphrey, C. and Thomas, H. (1983) 'Making efficient use of scarce resources', *Education*, August, p.125.

Humphrey, C. and Thomas, H. (1986) 'Delegating to schools', *Education*, 12 December, pp.513–14.

Inner London Education Authority (1977) *Keeping the School Under Review*, London.

Inner London Education Authority (1985) *Improving Primary Schools. Report of the Committee on Primary Education*, chaired by Norman Thomas, London.

Jones, A. (1987) *Leadership for Tomorrow's Schools*, Basil Blackwell, Oxford.

Joseph, K. (1984) *Speech to the North of England Education Conference*, 6 January, Sheffield.

Joseph, K. (1985) *Speech to the North of England Education Conference*, 4 January, Chester.

Kemp, R. and Nathan, M. (1990) *Middle Management in Schools: A Survival Guide*, Blackwell, Oxford.

Knight, B. (1989) *Managing School Time*, Longman, London.

Leiberman, N.M. (1956) *Education as a Profession*, Prentice Hall, New York.

Lawley, P. (1988) *Deputy Headship*, Longman, London.

Lewin, K. (1947) 'Force field analysis', *Human Relations*, vol.1, no.1, pp.5–41.

Lyons G. and Stenning, R. (1986) *Managing Staff in Schools: A Handbook*, Hutchinson, London.

McClelland, D.C. (1961) *The Achieving Society*, Van Nostrand, New York.

Maclure, S. (1989) 'Headship in perspective', *Education*, October, pp.11–12.

Marland, M. (ed.) (1986) *School Management Skills*, Heinemann Educational Books, London.

Marland, M. and Hill, S. (1981) *Departmental Management*, Heinemann Educational Books, London.

Maslow, A.H. (1954) *Motivation and Personality*, Harper & Row, New York.

Matthew, R. and Tong, S. (1982) *The Role of the Deputy Head in the Comprehensive School*, Ward Lock, London.

Merson, M. (1989) 'Teacher match and educational policy', *Journal of Educational Policy*, vol. 4, no. 2, pp.171–84.

Midwinter, E. (1985) 'Parents' role in teacher appraisal', *Times Educational Supplement*, 8 February.

Millerson, G. (1964) *The Qualifying Associations*, Routledge & Kegan Paul, London.

Mintzberg, H. (1973) *The Nature of Managerial Work*, Harper & Row, New York.

Morgan, C. (1981) *The Selection and Promotion of Staff*, Course E323, Management and the School, Block 6, The Management of Staff, Open University Press, Milton Keynes.

Morgan, C., Hall, V. and Mackay, H. (1983) *The Selection of Secondary School Headteachers*, Open University Press, Milton Keynes.

Morgan, C., Hall, V. and Mackay, H. (1984) *A Handbook on Selecting Senior Staff in Schools*, Open University Press, Milton Keynes.

Musgrove, F. and Taylor, P. (1969) *Society and the Teachers' Role*, Routledge & Kegan Paul, London.

National Curriculum Council (1989) *Information Pack Number 1*, NCC, York.

National Foundation for Educational Research (1989) *The Recruitment, Retention, Motivation and Morale of Senior Staff in Schools*, NFER, Slough.

Nias, J. (1980) 'Leadership styles and job satisfaction in primary schools', in Bush *et al.* (1980) *Approaches to School Management*, pp.225–73.

Nicholson, R. (1989) *School Management. The Role of the Secondary Headteacher*, Kogan Page, London.

Owen, P.R., Davies, M. and Wayment, A. (1983) 'The role of the deputy head in secondary schools', in P. Harling, *New Directions in Educational Leadership*, pp.247–52.

Paisey, A. (1984) 'Trends in educational leadership thought', in P. Harling (ed.) pp.25–37

Peters, T.S. and Waterman, R.H. (1982) *In Search of Excellence*, Harper & Row, London.

Poster, C. (1976) *School Decision-Making*, Heinemann Educational Books, London.

Poster, C. and Poster, D. (1991) *Teacher Appraisal: A Guide to Training*, Routledge, London.

Pountney, G. (1985) *Management in Action*, Longman Resource Unit for SCDC Publications, York.

Preedy, M. (1988) *Approaches to Curriculum Management, Block 3 of E325 Managing Schools*, Open University Press, Milton Keynes.

Reed, B. and Hall, J. (1989) *The School: Change and Challenge, Module 1: LEAP*, Local Education Authorities Project, Milton Keynes.

Reid K., Hopkins, D. and Holly, P. (1987) *Towards the Effective School*, Basil Blackwell, Oxford.

Ribbins, P. (1988) 'The role of the middle manager in the secondary school', in R. Glatter, M. Preedy, C. Riches and M. Masterton (1988) (eds) *Understanding School Management*, Open University Press, Milton Keynes.

Riches, C. (1988) *Management Roles and Responsibilities: The Secondary School, E325, Block 2, Part 3*, Open University Press, Milton Keynes.

Rust, W.B. (1985) *Management Guidelines for Teachers*, Pitman, London.

Sanday, A. (1990) *Making Schools More Effective*, CEDAR Papers, University of Warwick.

Scot, B. (1981) *The Skills of Negotiating*, Gower, Aldershot.

Shipman, M. (1979) *In-School Evaluation*, Heinemann Educational Books, London.

Simkins, T. and Thomas, H. (eds) (1987) *Economics and the Management of Education: Emerging Themes*, Falmer Press, London.

Styan, D. (1989a) *Times Educational Supplement*, 27 January.

Styan, D. (1989b) *Interim Report of the School Management Task Force*, DES, London.

Styan, D., Bailey, T., Foreman, K., Page, R. and Pitt, G. (1990) *Developing School Management: The Way Forward. A Report by the School Management Task Force*, HMSO, London.

Tannenbaum, R. and Schmidt, W. (1958) 'How to choose a leadership pattern', *Harvard Business Review*, vol.51, no.3, pp.162–75 and 178–80.

Tomlinson, J. (1986) *Crossing the Bridge: Addresses to the North of England Conferences*, Sheffield Papers in Educational Management No.54, Sheffield City Polytechnic, Sheffield.

Tomlinson, J.R.G. (1987) 'The purpose of primary education', The opening address to the *National Conference on Primary Education*, Scarborough, April.

Torington, D. and Weightman, J. (1989a) *The Reality of School Management*, Blackwell, Oxford.

Torrington, D. & Weightman, J. (1989b) *Management and Organisation in Secondary Schools: A Training Handbook*, Blackwell, Oxford.

Trethowan, D.M. (1984) *Delegation*, Education for Industrial Society, London.

Trethowan, D.M. (1987) *Appraisal and Target Setting: A Handbook for Teacher Development*, Harper & Row, London.

Warwick, D. (1983) *Staff Appraisal*, Education for Industrial Society, London.

Winecoff, L. and Powell, C. (1979) *Seven Steps to Educational Problem Solving*, Pendall Publishing Company, Midland, Michigan.

Wirrall Metropolitan Borough (1986) *Staff Training Profile and School Curriculum Expertise Profile, Primary Education*, Department of Education Municipal Offices, Birkenhead.

Woodcock, M. (1979) *Team Development Manual*, Gower, Aldershot.

Index

academic functions, of heads of
departments 34
acceptance of change 160
accountability, management by 6–7
achievement, need for 54
action: communication and 85; for
implementation of change 157–8;
planning and 151
action grids 158, 159
Adair, J. 40, 55, 75
Adams, N. 11
administration 19, 31, 74
affiliation, need for 54
agendas, for meetings 97, 101–2, 103
aims: and school management 20–4; of
staff teams 49–50; statement of 58,
59, 60, 62
analysis, and management of change
152–3
appraisal *see* staff appraisal
appraisal interview 136–9, 142
Aspects of Secondary Education 14
assessment 1, 6, 9, 11, 28
audit 60, 61, 62–4

Bell, L.A. 4, 31, 127
Blanchard, T. 6
body language 89–90
brainstorming 155, 157
budgets, management of 7, 29, 58, 63–4

Campbell, R.J. 15
chairpersons, of meetings 102–3
change: management of 148–50,
153–63; planning and 150–2
Clarke, Kenneth 126, 128
classroom observation 132–6
Cockroft Report (on teaching of

mathematics in schools) 35
collegial authority 29, 42, 46
commanding, as a management skill 37
commitment: to change 161; to pupils
41; to a team 29, 47–8, 52, 53
communication 38, 55, 83, 84–105;
effective 86–9; face-to-face 90–4; and
management of change 161;
meetings and 96–105; visual 95–6;
within teams 44, 74; written 94–5
conceptual management tasks 17
consensus, management by 6
controlling, as a management skill 37
co-ordinating, as a management skill
19, 37, 58
Coulson, A.A. 39
Cowan, B. 144
curriculum 28, 35; aims of 21; audit of
63; deputy heads and 33; *see also*
National Curriculum
curriculum content 1, 4
curriculum management 8–9, 16–17
Curriculum Matters 2 110–11
curriculum profiles 107–13, 123; of
schools 111, 113; of staff 108–11

Day, C. 28
Dean, J. 116
decision-making 37, 40; involvement in
40, 165; meetings for 99
delegation 56, 69, 80–3; by
headteachers 11, 81, 83; as a
management skill 13, 37, 44, 74; and
staff development 81, 145
deputy heads 5, 13, 30; job description
for 117–19, 120–1; role of 31–5
diagnosis of problems 153, 155
Drucker, P. 15–16, 36

Education Act, 1986 6, 17
Education Reform Act, 1988 6, 10, 17, 20, 21; and change in headteachers' role 31
Education (School Teachers' Pay and Conditions) Order 2, 37
efficiency, demands for 4
employers, as stakeholders in a school 20
evaluation 38, 68; of lessons 134, 135; of results of change 162–43
Everard, K.B. 20, 80, 105, 113
external management tasks 11, 18, 19, 166

face-to-face communication 90–4
Fayol, H. 36
Field, D. 16, 18
flexibility 24
force field maps 152–3, 154

GCSE, target setting and 78–9
Georgiades, N.J. 71
Good Teachers 1–2, 3, 36
Goodworth, C.T. 116
governing bodies 6, 10–11, 30, 32; and the curriculum 17; powers of 6–7, 29; reports to 30; and staff selection 123; and statement of aims 59

Hall, J. 21
Handy, C. 25, 41
Hargreaves, D. 60, 63, 64, 68, 70
heads of department 5, 14, 18, 30; functions of 34–6
headteachers 1, 14, 18, 23, 148; appraisal of 125, 126; changing roles of 31; as chief executives 7, 30; conditions of employment of 2–3; delegation by 11, 81, 83; and external relations 18; and governing bodies 30; and school development plans 59, 64; and staff selection 119, 122; and staff teams 45
Heller, H. 150
Her Majesties Inspectorate 13, 14, 22–3, 26, 34
Hoyle, E. 29, 38, 41
Hughes, M. 18, 36
human relations management tasks 18

implementation: of change 160–1; of

school development plan 68–71
industrial relations 32
industry, involvement with 32
information: collection of 144, 155, 156; from meetings 97–8
innovation 19, 74
in-service training (INSET) 4, 14–15, 79, 81–2; meetings for 99; staff appraisal and 128, 129, 130; staff development and 143–5
interpersonal skills 36
isolation, of teachers 14, 15, 107

jargon, use of in written communication 94, 95
job descriptions 108, 113–21, 123
Jones, A. 10, 58
Joseph, Sir Keith 127

Lawley, P. 32
leadership in schools 38–41, 42; see also team leaders
LEAs (local education authorities) 6, 20; financial statements from 30; meeting training needs 130; and staff appraisal 125
Leiberman, N.M. 41
lessons, appraisal of 134–5
Lewin, K. 152
listening, and communication 91, 92, 93–4
LMS (local management of schools) 10, 17
Lyons, G. 116

McClelland, D.C. 54
Maclure, S. 31
MacGregor, John 126
Maher, P. 4
management 10, 11, 13, 15; of change 148–63; new approaches to 4–6; tasks of 15–19
management skills 11, 36–8
managerial function, of heads of department 35
marketing 33, 166–7
Marland, M. 3, 35
Maslow, A.H. 53
Matthew, R. 31
meetings 32, 36; organising 96–7, 100–5; purposes of 97–100
middle management 10, 14, 23, 25, 45,

74; development of 5, 7, 58; role of 18, 34–6; *see also* team leaders
Midwinter, E. 128
Millerson, G. 41
minutes, of meetings 103–4
mismatch 9
monitoring: as a management skill 38; of tasks in change process 161–3
Morgan, C. 16
Morris, G. 20, 80, 105
motivating: as a management skill 37, 68; staff appraisal and 128
Musgrove, F. 41

National Curriculum 4, 6, 11, 33, 108; aims of 8; and curriculum audit 63; implementation of 9; management of 8–9
National Curriculum Council 6
National Foundation for Educational Research 30, 33
national standards 4
National Steering Group, recommendations of, for staff appraisal 125–6, 127
needs, of team members 53–4
Nias, J. 39
Nicholson, R. 33, 34
non-teaching time, allocation of 14
notice boards, use of, for communication 95–6

objectives: of lessons 26, 134; of meetings 100; of school development plans 61; setting of 36; of staff teams 50, 51, 53, 55; in statement of aims 23
observation, in the classroom 131–6
open enrolment 6, 10
organisation of schools 13
organising, as a management skill 37
Owen, P.R. 32

Paisley, A. 39
parents 6, 10–11, 29; contact with 32; reports to 70; and staff appraisal 128
pastoral care 5, 13, 17, 23
performance criteria 83
performance indicators, for lessons 134–5
person specifications 121–3
Peters, T.S. 25, 26

Phillimore, L. 71
planning 37, 55; for change 51, 150–2, 158; for meetings 97; for staff development 144; *see also* school development plans
Poster, C. 10, 107, 127
Poster, D. 127
Pountney, G. 162
preparation, for lessons 134
primary school liaison 8, 33
priorities: identification of in school development plans 66–7, 68, 73; of staff teams 74
problem-solving 99, 144, 155
professional autonomy, of teachers 41, 42, 129
professional development *see* staff development
professional leadership 19, 28, 31
profiling *see* curriculum profiles
progress checking 69–70
project work, for staff development 144
public relations 30, 31
pupils 20, 22, 23, 162; and development planning 70; learning of 132–3, 134; numbers of 4; welfare of 33

questioning, and communication 91, 93

Read, B. 21
Reid, K. 24
religious education 6
reporting 18, 70, 79, 144; from governing bodies 29, 30
representative functions, of heads of departments 35
resistance to change 149–50, 151
resource allocation 4, 24, 51, 74, 165–6
resource management 1, 5, 10, 14, 31, 34, 166
resources: audit of 63–4; for staff appraisal 130–1
responsibilities of teachers 2–3; division of 109, 110; job descriptions and 113, 116
Ribbins, P. 34
Riches, C. 31
Rust, W.B. 41

salvation 19, 74
Schmidt, W. 39

school buildings 32–3
school development plans 17, 18, 58–60, 77; benefits of 59–60; as a cyclical process 60–2, 71; constructing 67; implementing 68–71; staff development and 141–2
school effectiveness 23–7
school governors see governing bodies
school inspectors 33, 122
schools: performance of 111, 113; profiles of 123; size of and management style 4–5
Schools Examination and Assessment Council 6
science 4, 9
senior management teams 1, 5, 7, 11, 20, 58, 73
Shaw, George Bernard 148
Simkins, T. 3, 4
stability, of staff teams 163–7
staff appraisal 56, 125–31, 164; benefits of 137; in class-room observation 131–6; interview for 136–39; preparation for 138; and school development 141–2
staff development 18, 141–8; appraisal and 127, 128–29, 139; and delegation 80; deputy heads and 34, 35; headteachers and 31; school development and 61, 67, 141–2; staff teams and 45, 56, 74; strategies for 144, 146, 149; team leaders and 28–9, 38
staff teams 10, 12, 28; brainstorming sessions in 155, 157; communication within 86–7, 94; confidence of, in leader 164–5; development of 48–57, 74, 102; management of 44–5; and management of change 73, 151, 152, 153, 160; marketing of 167–8; members of 36, 46, 52–3, 54, 107; nature of 46–8; stability of 163, 164–7; target setting of 75–80
staffing audit 64, 65
staffing structure 13
stakeholders, in schools 10, 20–1
statement of aims 20–3, 58, 59, 60, 62
statutory orders 9
Stenning, R. 116
Styan, D. 3, 11, 12, 13
subject departments, heads of see heads of department

Tannenbaum, R. 39
targets 68, 73, 75–80; setting of 55, 75–6, 77; types of 76
task achievement 40, 42, 51, 61, 78
tasks: delegation of 81–3; and school development plans 67; of staff teams 49, 50, 51–2, 55, 78–80
Taylor, P. 41
teachers 1–2, 23; appraisal of see staff appraisal; classroom observation of 131–6; and external relations 18; incompetent 127–8; involvement of, in statement of aims 9, 20, 25; job descriptions for 113–21; management of 2, 41–3; management responsibilities of 2, 3, 12, 15, 19; and National Curriculum 9; as a profession 41; profiles of 108–10; selection of 17, 32, 35, 42; valuing of 164; see also staff development; staff teams
Teaching Quality 128
teaching skills 134
team leaders 46–7, 165, 166, 167; communication by 86, 88, 92–3, 105; delegation by 81, 83; and development of team 48, 50, 52, 55–6, 163–4; and management of change 150, 152, 155, 158, 160, 161–3; at meetings 99, 100, 102–3; and resource allocation 166; role of, in staff development 28–9, 38, 141, 146–7, 148; and school development plans 68–9; and school effectiveness 24; setting targets 80, 81; and time management 74–5
teamwork 2, 10, 11, 29, 34, 43; benefits of 46; management through 44–57; see also staff teams
technical and executive functions 18–19, 31
technical management tasks 16–17
Ten Good Schools 13, 30
Thomas, H. 3, 4
time: lack of 14; management of 51–2, 74–5, 105
Tomlinson, J.R.G. 163
Tong, S. 31
Torrington, D. 32, 163, 164
transition management 158
Trethowan, D.M. 76, 77
TVEI 4, 5, 14, 18

verbal communication 84, 90–4
videos, for communication 96
visits, staff development and 144
visual aids 96, 102;
visual communication 84, 95–6

Waterman, R.H. 25, 26
Weightman, J. 32, 163, 164
Wright, N. 143
written communication 84, 94–5